Third Edition

The
Power to
Communicate

SO-ART-897

Third Edition

The Power to Communicate

Gender Differences as Barriers

Deborah Borisoff
New York University

Lisa Merrill
Hofstra University

WAVELAND PRESS, INC.
Prospect Heights, Illinois

For information about this book, write or call:
    Waveland Press, Inc.
    P.O. Box 400
    Prospect Heights, Illinois 60070
    (847) 634-0081

About the Authors

Deborah Borisoff, Ph.D., is an Associate Professor of Speech Communication in the Department of Culture and Communication at New York University. In the communication area, Dr. Borisoff has published multiple journal articles, contributed numerous book chapters, and written a number of books, including *Conflict Management: A Communication Skills Approach*, with David A. Victor, *Listening in Everyday Life: A Personal & Professional Approach*, coedited with Michael Purdy, and *Women and Men Communicating: Challenges and Changes*, coedited with Laurie P. Arliss. She has served as a consultant to corporations, government agencies, and educational institutions. Professor Borisoff recently served as President of the Eastern Communication Association (ECA). Awards received include Distinguished Research Fellow, Distinguished Teaching Fellow, and the ECA Past Officers' Club Award.

Lisa Merrill, Ph.D., is an Associate Professor in the Department of Speech Communication and Rhetorical Studies at Hofstra University. Dr. Merrill's research and publications focus on the construction of gender, intercultural communication issues in performance studies, nonverbal communication, mass media, psychotherapy, and pedagogy. She has lectured widely in India, Egypt, and Ireland. Her most recent publications on gender and communication are her critical biography of nineteenth-century American actress Charlotte Cushman, *When Romeo Was a Woman*, and the upcoming anthology, *Untying the Tongue: Power, Gender, and the Word*, co-edited with Linda Longmire. Dr. Merrill is a registered drama therapist (R.D.T.); she also leads workshops on cultural diversity, teambuilding, and gender issues in the workplace.

Contents

Preface   xi

**Introduction:
Changing Terms for Changing Times**   **1**

Chapter One   **The Stereotype: Fiction or Fact**   **5**
Feminine Stereotypes 6
  Background   6
  Limitations of the Feminine Stereotype   10
Masculine Stereotypes 12
  Background   12
  Limitations of the Male Stereotype   13
Nonverbal Aspects of the Stereotypes 16
Suggested Activities   17

Chapter Two   **Vocal and Verbal Behaviors**   **19**
Vocal Behaviors 20
  Articulation, or "How correct do you sound?"   20
  Pitch, or "How big do you sound?"   23
  Intonation, or "How certain do you sound?"   25
Verbal Constructs 28
  Qualifiers, or "I sort of think maybe you know
    what I mean," and Intensifiers, or "I'm sooo
    very, very glad to hear it"   29
  Disclaimers, or "This probably doesn't mean
    anything, but . . ."   30

Tag Questions, or "This is what I meant, isn't it?" 31

Compound Requests, or "How many words shall I use to make my wishes known?" 33

Vocabulary Differences, or "Which words are whose?" 34

Verbal and Vocal Behaviors in Interaction 35

Talk Time 36

Topic Initiation and Topic Selection 37

Self-Disclosure 38

Interruptions and Overlaps 40

Vocalizers and Minimal Responses 42

Accounting for the Communicative Behaviors: Difference or Dominance? 43

Suggested Activities 47

Chapter Three   Gender and Nonverbal Communication   51

Space, or "Bigger Is Better" 52

Touch, or "Just a Friendly Pat on the Back?" 55

Height, or "Whom Do You Look Up To?" 57

Facial Expressions, or "You Look So Pretty When You Smile" 58

Gaze, or "Are You Looking at Me?" 61

Gesture and Demeanor, or "Act Like a Lady" 63

Artifactual Messages, or "What You Wear Speaks Volumes" 63

Decoding Nonverbal Messages, or "I Can See What You Mean" 64

Suggested Activities 66

Chapter Four   Gendered Scripts: Early Socialization in the Home and School   69

The Influence of Dualism on Shaping Thought 70

Socialization: Reinforcing Attitudes about Sex-Traits and Sex-Roles 72

Educational Practices: A Different Experience for Males and Females 80

Teaching Style 80

Assumptions about Student Performance 83

Suggested Activities 86

Chapter Five   **Gendered Scripts: Women and Men**
in the Workplace   89
Gender Stereotyping: Maintaining the Myth
of "Women's Work" and "Men's Work"   90
Hiring Practices: How Appearances Are
"Read" by Employers   92
Salary Practices: Maintaining Economic
Disparities 95
Gender in the Workplace: Questioning
Differences in Professional Performance   97
Sexual Harassment:
Communicating Domination   102
Child Care: Maintaining Differences in
Responsibility   109
Gender in the "Virtual" Office   115
Suggested Activities   118

Chapter Six   **Changing the Gendered Scripts**   **119**
Effecting Change:
Expanding Human Potential   119

References   **123**

Index   **143**

Preface

This book addresses two essential issues that are often missing from works that deal with communication. First, it examines the impact of the stereotyped gender differences that are so powerful a force in male and female development, in communication, and in male and female professional contexts.

Second, this book includes strategies and techniques that may be helpful to both women and men in dealing with persistent traditional attitudes and in attempting to break from them.

Chapter 1 examines the prevalent stereotypes traditionally associated with masculinity and femininity and suggests how assumptions about gendered behavior may inhibit *human* communication. In chapters 2 and 3, we explore how the construction of gender may be manifested in women's and men's vocal, verbal, and nonverbal communication, in both personal and professional contexts. We indicate, moreover, how these behaviors frequently are construed by others. Chapter 4 considers the extent to which early socialization and education undergird and often reinforce divergent expectations for women and men. We explain in chapter 5 how these different expectations may be reinforced in the work world and in the home. How we may begin to alter the gendered scripts is the focus of chapter 6.

Following each of the first five chapters, we have provided numerous activities and exercises that can be used in a variety of instructional and training situations. These activities have been created to target both communication skills, such as listening ability and conflict resolution, and settings, such as one-to-one dyads, small group situations, and public communication contexts.

Introduction

Changing Terms for Changing Times

Nearly every decade can be singled out for special achievements or strides. The last two decades of the twentieth century are no exception—especially in the area of accomplishments by women. During the initial years of this period, for the first time a woman was appointed to the Supreme Court, served as a member of a space mission, and was nominated as a vice-presidential candidate for a major U.S. party.

While advancements in the area of technology are clearly apparent, social changes are more difficult to assess, often requiring the distance of decades—in some instances, centuries. Although differences in the behaviors expected of either sex have always existed, the explanations offered for these disparities have changed over time. For example, a century ago, it was argued that women were physiologically ill-suited to intellectual endeavors and that higher education was not only "unladylike"—it would adversely affect women's reproductive abilities. At the present time, few would argue that women are biologically unfit for these pursuits. This example demonstrates a shift in perspective about the deterministic role played by biology. Thus the behaviors of and traits associated with men and women discussed in this text are referred to as "gender" rather than "sex" differences because they are socially constructed and not innate.

When we wrote the first two editions of this book (1985, 1992), we took it for granted that we, our readers, and the theorists and researchers whose work on gender and communication we cited shared relatively stable meanings for the terms that mark our common area of concern. *Communication*—the exchange of messages—was a

1

symbolic activity shaped and influenced by the dynamics and inequities of *power*; those with more socially sanctioned power dispro-
portionally controlled messages and meanings. Further, we had come
to see that messages and symbol systems did not just reflect the power
of those who used them, they helped construct and sustain the power
imbalance.

We recognized that while an explosion of empirical studies on
women's and men's communicative behavior and styles was underway,
perceptions of "appropriate" *gender*—rather than an individual's biological sex—seemed to account to a large degree for many of the
"differences" observed. We understood gender to be the socially constructed set of acts that were associated with, constitutive of, or
expected as indications of an individual's "femininity" or "masculinity"
in a given cultural setting. But beliefs about gender are not simple or
constant, as we've noted above. In disparate cultures, socioeconomic
classes, and time periods, different behaviors have been considered
"masculine" or "feminine." For example, in working-class white environments in the nineteenth-century United States, a physical,
muscular display of virility was part of the complex construction of
masculinity, but among more privileged social classes and for the British at the same time, "manliness" was associated with morality and
self-restraint (Bederman, 1995). At the same time, some women might
be complimented for their "manly" talents or condemned for "mannish" aspirations, while men who did not perform their social group's
expectation of masculinity were generally disparaged for being "effeminate." For not only were "men" and "women" expected and believed to
communicate differently from each other, these differences were differentially valued. Communicative behaviors associated with men and
masculinity (whether, in fact, they were performed by men or women)
were assumed to be better, a desirable norm against which all behaviors were judged.

Currently, as if to illustrate the historical contingency of accepted
notions of gender and communication, the very terms under which
much of communication research was conducted a decade ago have
been the source of debates that have transformed our area of inquiry
(Roman, Juhasz, and Miller, 1994). Many contemporary theorists now
avoid monolithic discussions of "women's" or "men's" communication.
Since neither "all men" nor "all women" are the same, using those
terms without accounting for other influences may imply a universality
that erases considerations of culture, socioeconomic class, ethnicity,
nationality, sexuality, and numerous other variables that, along with

gender, help "construct" our behavior. For many researchers the notion of *gender differences* is no longer unproblematic, since rigid and polarized categories are seen to exaggerate any differences and overshadow similarities between males and females, as well as to obscure whatever variation exists among women and among men (Canary and Hause, 1993; Henley and Kramarae, 1991, cited in Roman, Juhasz, and Miller,1994; Thorne, 1990).

In recent years, some theorists of "gender difference" have focused their attention on linguistic and psychological development, suggesting that our experiences of gender are largely constructed and shaped by language, since it is through the symbolic system of language that individuals develop a subjective sense of self. In this text we examine these changing beliefs and the impact they have on the messages we send and share with others. But change is never easy—particularly for those whose position of privilege is threatened. Furthermore, communication is a process many take for granted as though it were a "natural" individual expression and not a learned set of behaviors shaped by the larger cultural discourses which influence us all.

Yet with increasing numbers of women pursuing careers, and many men sharing more equally in the responsibilities of homes and families, both women and men are now expected to demonstrate communicative behavior that previously was thought to be the province of the "other" sex. They now must question the "meanings" that may have been taken for granted as they interpret the messages of others. These changes in behavior are easier to consider intellectually than they are to achieve because it is no small task to break from our prescribed cultural upbringing. It is necessary to understand and reevaluate stereotypes about communication and gender because the urge to maintain the *status quo* is powerful among many segments of our population while others are now striving for opportunities long denied them. Ideologies about gender are in flux, and it is important to untangle the contradictory discourses at play, such as when women who have been raised to be deferential to others are told to be aggressive to "succeed" in business, or when men who have been raised to regard homemaking as "women's work" are expected to share equally in the household chores. In both cases, a rethinking of traditional notions of male dominance is required, and this can be very hard to do.

Empirical research in the areas of speech communication, psychology, sociology, anthropology, and linguistics demonstrates the continuing perception of a difference in communication styles between women and men in the United States. Research has been conducted in a variety of areas that deal with communication and miscommunication between men and women. Sociological research has focused on the social roles performed by men and women and on the attitudes they communicate about relationships, work, money, and sex. The implications of language use as it affects the development and perceived roles of young children in society has been one focus of linguists. Nonverbal behavior as a powerful communication force and a gestural component of gender continues to attract the interest of scholars from a variety of academic disciplines. But much more needs to be done. Overwhelmingly, empirical studies examine the behaviors of small numbers of white, middle-class, heterosexual subjects (usually in university settings), and from these findings extend their application to "all women" or "all men." Far too infrequently do questions of ethnic difference, sexuality, or the impact of subjects' relative degrees of power enter into the interpretations or prescriptions of even the most well-meaning researchers.

In this book, we will consider communication styles, strategies, and behaviors and their relationships to gender stereotypes as well as the barriers these stereotypes impose on men and women. We will also explore some familial, educational, and occupational contexts in which gendered communication strategies are learned, performed, and sometimes, contested. By examining the connections between communication styles and gender we hope to provide a means to enrich and expand the communication behavior of both men and women. The rewards of such change may accrue not only in the professional arena but also in the area of personal relationships. Both sexes stand to benefit by such an understanding. Both will benefit from a more equal participation in the communication process.

Chapter One

The Stereotype
Fiction or Fact

Decorum utterly forbids each sex to model itself on the other, and that boldness of speech, demeanor, and conduct, so becoming to a man would be simply intolerable in a woman.

> — James McGrigor Allan, "Woman Suffrage
> Wrong in Principle, and Practice"

Power is the ability to take one's place in whatever discourse is essential to action and the right to have one's part matter.

> — Carolyn Heilbrun, *Writing a Woman's Life*

Public speaking is an assertive act. "Speech" and "voice" are frequently used as metaphors for power. It is in the act of giving voice to one's thoughts and feelings that a speaker has the potential to affect the thoughts and behavior of others. As anthropologist Susan Gal has noted (1994), "it is in part through verbal practices in social interaction that the structural relations of gender and dominance are perpetuated and sometimes subverted." Gal describes political assemblies, educational institutions, and courtrooms as occasions for verbal interaction and, therefore, as potential "site[s] of struggles about gender definitions and power . . . concern[ing] who can speak where about what" (p. 408).

Throughout much of recorded history, women have been forbidden to or actively discouraged from exercising their power of speech in public settings. Female silence has been equated with modesty, obedience, and womanly virtue (Keohane, 1981). Social and religious injunctions against women communicators have abounded. In the *New Testament*, Saint Paul instructed men to "Let a woman learn in silence

5

with all submissiveness." He said, "I permit no woman to teach or to have authority over men; she is to keep silent" (1 Timothy 2:9–15).

The authors of this text are both teachers; readers of this text presumably are enlightened *contemporary* women and men, yet all of us have been influenced by what historically has been considered *appropriate* communicative behavior for our respective sexes. In this chapter, we discuss the stereotypical expectations placed upon speakers of both sexes, some of the sanctions anticipated and endured by those who violate the expectations, and the process by which gender-based stereotypes have been internalized.

FEMININE STEREOTYPES

Background

In the 1650s, Anne Hutchinson was exiled from the Massachusetts Bay Colony because she attempted to have a voice in religious affairs. Hutchinson's "crime" was that she led meetings, called "conversations," in her home for groups of sixty or more people who came to listen to her theories about Christ. Her eloquent demeanor infuriated her accusers. John Winthrop, governor of the colony, described Hutchinson as "A Woman of a haughty and fierce carriage, of a nimble wit and active spirit and a very voluble tongue" (Prince Society Publications, 1894, p. 158). Hutchinson's ease and skill as a communicator were, in part, her crime, as was her usurpation of the male prerogative of speaking to an assembled audience. This violated the norms for acceptable womanly behavior. Women were not supposed to assume the authority of a public speaker, command the attention of an audience, or allow themselves to be the object of their spectators' gaze. Consequently, when they spoke in public, they were considered impious or immodest.

In anticipation of a negative reaction, some early women speakers chose to apologize to their audience for the uncharacteristic act. Priscilla Mason said in her salutatory oration at the Young Ladies' Academy of Philadelphia on May 15, 1793, "A female, young and inexperienced, addressing a promiscuous assembly is a novelty which requires an apology, as some may suppose. I therefore, with submission beg issue to offer a few thoughts on the vindication of female eloquence" (Berkin and Norton, 1979, pp. 89–90). Mason went on to propose that speech, even in public settings, need not be antithetical to current notions of femininity. However, most of Mason's eighteenth- and nineteenth-century contemporaries vociferously disagreed.

With the coming of industrialization in the nineteenth century, historians affirm that "role divisions and sexual stereotypes were permanently imprinted in the American popular mind" (Ryan, 1975, p. 75). The vast majority of licensed doctors and educators were male. Most of these men believed, and convinced the populace, that the female brain and internal organs would be injured by sustained intellectual effort. Nevertheless, women reformers, abolitionists, and women's rights activists embarked upon public speaking tours.

Two of the first American women to challenge successfully the notion that public speaking was unfeminine were abolitionists Sarah and Angelina Grimke. Daughters of a South Carolina slave-holding family, the Grimkes moved north to Philadelphia and joined the Quakers, the only large religious denomination in the nineteenth century to allow women to become ordained as ministers. The Grimkes were invited by the American Anti-Slavery Society to speak at what were to be small parlor gatherings of women in New York. At their first meeting, more than three hundred women showed up. On subsequent occasions, men attended as well, and the Grimkes were soon addressing mixed audiences. As with other women who were political activists, people were as much outraged by the audacity of a woman speaking to a mixed audience as they were offended by anything she might say. In a reaction against the Grimkes, the clergy published a pastoral letter from the Massachusetts Council of Congregational Ministers which asserted that, "When woman assumes the place and tone of man as a public reformer . . . she yields the power which God has given her for protection, and her character becomes unnatural" (*The Liberator*, 1837).

Increasingly throughout the nineteenth century, other American women risked being regarded as "unnatural" as they stood up to speak out on such social and political issues as abolition, temperance, women's right to education, and women's right to vote. In fact, the movement for women's rights in the United States was, from the beginning, intimately tied to the struggle by women to speak out on their own behalf.

In 1840, when American abolitionists Lucretia Mott and Elizabeth Cady Stanton met in London at the World Anti-Slavery Convention, they were mortified to find that women were not allowed to participate in the proceedings and were forced to sit passively behind a curtain. These women who had worked so courageously for the abolitionist cause were denied the right to speak at the convention to which they and their spouses had been invited. As a result of this outrage, they vowed to organize a convention that would protest against what Stanton called "the injustice which had brooded for ages over the character and destiny of half the human race" (Martin, 1972, p. 42). The denial of speech was a paradigm for the other injustices women suffered. Eight years later, Stanton and Mott led the Seneca Falls Convention. Most historians cite this event as the origin of the organized women's movement in the United States.

Even on this momentous occasion, the prejudice against women communicators was as strong as the reaction to the speakers' message. Stanton's husband, abolitionist Henry B. Stanton, threatened to leave town if Elizabeth delivered a speech in which she proposed demanding the vote for women. Henry Stanton did leave town, and the long, scholarly, eloquent speech that Elizabeth Cady Stanton delivered was prefaced by an apology. Stanton said to her audience, "I should feel exceedingly diffident to appear before you at this time, having never before spoken in public, were I not nerved by a sense of right and duty, did I not feel the time had fully come for the question of women's wrongs to be laid before the public, did I not believe that woman herself must do this work; for woman alone can understand the height, the depth, the length, and the breadth of her own degradation. Man cannot speak for her" (cited in Dubois, 1981, p. 28). Stanton's purported "diffidence" was understandable given that many of her contemporaries believed that a woman speaking publicly was compromising her modesty, purity, and virtue. The women of Stanton's time were expected to "noiselessly" follow their husband's lead.

Nonetheless, there were a few notable exceptions. Stanton's contemporary, activist Lucy Stone, was one of the earliest American women who deliberately planned to undertake a career as a public speaker. After graduating from Oberlin College in 1847, Stone became a professional antislavery lecturer. In 1855, when Stone married fellow abolitionist Henry Blackwell, the *Boston Post* published a poem that ended, "A name like Curtius' shall be his/on Fame's loud trumpet blown/ who with a wedding kiss shuts up/ the mouth of Lucy Stone" (Flexner, 1968, p. 70). Fortunately, the Blackwell-Stone marriage appears to have been a union in which Blackwell supported and encouraged Stone's activism and public speaking. However, implicit in the anonymous verse published in the *Post* was the belief that husbands may "shut up" their wives and that women who talk too much should be silenced.

Sojourner Truth, an eloquent speaker who had been born into slavery, challenged the predominant mid-nineteenth-century view that the restrictions and prohibitions women encountered in the public realm were benevolent, enacted for their own protection. In a stirring speech entitled "Arn't I A Woman?," delivered at an 1851 women's rights convention, Truth recounted her own experiences as a former slave and as a woman who had "worked as hard as men, born the lash as well" and had "never been helped into carriages" (Truth, 1878). Women of color and poor women were even less likely to gain access to public expression than were white, middle-class women activists.

Political scientist Nannerl O. Keohane (1981) has asserted that, "The power of such prescriptive silence is such that when women do speak, their speech sounds strange. It deviates from the norm of masculinity in timbre and in pattern. . . . And the words of women are consistently devalued in group settings, not heard, assumed to be trivial, not attended to" (pp. 91–92). Unlike the women activists mentioned above, the *stereotypically* feminine speaker—against whom assertive female public speakers continue to be judged—is soft spoken, self-effacing, and compliant. Considered more emotional than logical, she is prone to be seen as disorganized and subjective.

It is obvious that this image of women is biased and restrictive, as are all stereotypes. Yet, despite all evidence to the contrary, stereotypes tend to be believed because they serve a social purpose, perpetuating the power relationships in a given society. Linguist Julia Penelope (1990) describes the following stereotypical features associated with women's speech as "a dialect some women use, and only in specific contexts, to signal recognition and acceptance of their subordinate status" (p. xxi). You may wonder why anyone in this day and age would choose, however unintentionally, to signal his/her relative powerlessness to others. Rather than any reflection of a "natural" tendency on the part of female speakers, the hyperpolite dialect that is constitutive of femininity can be considered a "protective verbal facade, a means of self-defense" (Penelope 1990, p. xxiii), a strategy born of gender role training in a patriarchal culture which associates femininity with submissiveness. Let us look in greater detail at these limitations in the feminine stereotype.

Limitations of the Feminine Stereotype

She is soft spoken. Women, like children, have been taught that it is preferable for them to be seen rather than to be heard. When heard, female voices are apt to be considered abrasive or displeasing, and their words devoid of serious meaning.

If we examine some of the more pejorative adjectives that can be used to describe speakers, we see that in addition to Hutchinson's "voluble" tongue, a voice may be considered carping, brassy, nagging, shrill, strident, or grating. Conversing may be referred to as babbling, blabbing, gabbing, or chattering. Although these terms are not specifically gender-identified, they are commonly used to describe the speech behavior of females; each implies the superficial or trivial nature of the speaker's message. Many women have internalized this socially imposed stereotype; in many cases, a deeply rooted reticence to speaking out precludes them from expressing themselves in any public setting, rather than risk being judged in such negative terms.

Sociologist Lucille Duberman (1975) has explained that "to internalize means . . . to adopt the standards of one's society as part of one's self image, so that the attitudes and behaviors approved by the society appear to have no possible alternatives" (p. 27). By accepting and internalizing the stereotypical view of women as communicators, women are discouraged from using their voice to assert a point strongly. The soft-spoken woman's voice does not carry. She threatens no one; she may lack sufficient force and volume to speak up effectively and convincingly. Women who are hampered by the need to sound "feminine" may adopt a high-pitched "little girl" voice, an artificially "sexy," breathy voice, or a volume so low as to be barely audible. In any case, the "soft spoken" woman is at a marked disadvantage if she attempts to negotiate a contract, persuade a jury, or present a report.

She is self-effacing. Some theorists, following Robin Lakoff (1975), claim that women's messages are ignored, interrupted, and not attended to because women are taught to "talk like a lady"—to use disclaimers ("This may not be right, but . . ."), "weak" particles ("Dear me," "Goodness," etc.) rather than forceful expletives, and tag questions ("The book was good, wasn't it?") and to reflect uncertainty rather than assertiveness. When women do not employ these tactics, they may be accused of being unfeminine; however, if they do "talk like a lady," they risk not being taken seriously. Other linguists, such as Deborah Cameron (1992) question whether the "folklinguistic" profile described by Lakoff accurately reflects most women's speech behavior at all. Yet the belief persists that one of the ways women may perform their femininity is to adopt communicative strategies that are hyperpolite, constructed to please others by minimizing one's own skills, rather than to risk antagonizing one's (presumably male/more powerful) audience. When women do adopt these tactics, the perception of women's relative weakness as communicators is confirmed.

She is compliant. The diffidence or insecurity experienced by the speaker who is conscious of her violation of societal norms may be manifested in several ways. Rather than be labeled "unnatural" or "unfeminine," a woman may engage in what Janet Stone and Jane Bachner (1977) have called "self-trivializing messages" that register the speaker's insecurity, doubt, and eagerness to please.

The compliant speaker allows herself to be interrupted. She moves out of the way when someone approaches her. She smiles often to assure the good will of others. She maintains eye contact and listens attentively while others speak but averts her eyes when she is the focus of attention. The compliant woman demonstrates her submissiveness through these communicative behaviors, which are characteristics of subordinates in a hierarchy. Those who are perceived, and who perceive themselves, as less powerful tend to employ verbal and nonverbal tactics calculated to appease rather than to threaten their listeners. Because of the pervasiveness of gender hierarchies, women who do not engage in these behaviors have often been criticized.

She is emotional and subjective. This aspect of the feminine stereotype directly affects the female speaker's credibility. A speaker is considered credible when she or he can demonstrate competence, dynamism, consistency, and coorientation with an audience. Yet many listeners accept what mathematician Evelyn Fox Keller (1983) identifies as a patriarchal dichotomy which regards "objectivity, reason, and mind as male, and subjectivity, feeling and nature as female" (p. 15). Although feminist and phenomenological researchers in a wide range of disciplines have illustrated the fallacy of supposedly objective, value-free research, many audiences still regard as less credible a message which acknowledges the subjective experience of a speaker rather than relying on "facts" assembled in such a way as to negate the speaker's role in his or her presentation. We have been taught to view objectivity as superior to subjectivity. This is part of the lens through which women and men have been taught to view the world. Simone de Beauvoir (1952) wrote that "representation of the world, like the world itself, is the work of men. They describe it from their own point of view, which they confuse with the absolute truth" (p. 133). It is from this "truth" that our masculine and feminine stereotypes have evolved.

MASCULINE STEREOTYPES

Background

Historically, men have had almost exclusive access to formal language training and to education. In the Judeo-Christian tradition, men learned and spoke Hebrew and Latin. One of the dicta of Rabbinic Judaism was, "cursed be the man who teaches his daughter Torah" (Ruether, 1981, p. 52). In religion, politics, and education, men were afforded the right and given the encouragement to learn, to speak what they knew, and to use their speech to achieve their desires.

Rhetoric, the formal study of oral discourse as a means of persuasion and of finding "truth" is one of the oldest academic disciplines. Originating in the Western world with the Greeks, rhetoric was based upon masculine communication models. Walter J. Ong (1972) wrote that, "Rhetoric developed in the past as a major expression of the rational level of ceremonial combat which is found among males and typically only among males at the physical level throughout the entire animal kingdom" (p. 128). Ong claimed that not only was the masculine model of communication based on confrontation and conflict, but that academic education (which for centuries was the exclusive province of males until the romantic age) was consequently based on "defending a position (thesis) or attacking the position of another person" (1972, p. 128). All disciplines were taught by this method.

The masculine model is that of a speaker who is direct, confrontative, forceful, and logical. His few, well-chosen words are focused on making a particular point.

In Western societies, men have been reared to confront, to compete, to challenge, and to win; women have been taught to acquiesce, to accommodate, and to compromise. When placed within the framework of communication, this gender-linked behavior leads males to gravitate toward delivering organized public speeches and debates, while women are encouraged to mediate and to listen. In most cultures, implicit in this division of tasks is a hierarchy of values.

Western males have been taught to be logical, objective, and impersonal; women have been encouraged to be subjective, self-disclosing, and personal. Overwhelmingly, the "masculine" traits have been afforded greater status. Women render themselves vulnerable by their self-disclosure; men derive power from sounding authoritative and communicating facts rather than emotions. Daniel Maltz and Ruth Borker (1982) contend that men's speech is a vehicle for male displays of power—"a power based on the larger social order but reinforced and expressed in face-to-face interaction with women" (pp. 198–99).

Many communication texts reinforce the masculine model of communication by employing aggressive metaphors in their discussion of rhetoric. Speakers are instructed to "arm" themselves against the other speaker's "argument"; to "win" their point by "waging an attack" on the "weak" points in their "opponent's" logic with a strong "plan of battle." Both war and sports metaphors encourage speakers to think of communication as combative, a contest that one wins or loses.

There are major drawbacks to this reliance on stereotyped "masculinity." First, unlike the specifically "feminine" stereotypes, the "masculine" stereotype *appears to be neutral* rather than gender specific. Simone de Beauvoir has explained that masculine values and behavior have been considered the desirable "human" norm, while values and behavior associated with women have been regarded as aberrant and "other" (1952, p. xvi). It is, therefore, often difficult for men to see that the male generic is, in fact, the "male-specific." Consequently, men have resisted identifying the limitations of their role and expanding upon it. The limitations in the "feminine" stereotype as we have identified it are explicit. However, we need to dig deeper to uncover the negative implications in the male role.

Limitations of the Male Stereotype

He is an ineffective listener. One deficiency in the masculine stereotype has been the negative association for listening. As we have established, speaking is active. Listening has often been portrayed inaccurately as passive, weak, or "feminine" behavior, since it necessitates receptivity to others. Because much of their survival has depended upon the ability to read and decode accurately the verbal and nonverbal clues of superiors, women (and other subordinates in hierarchies) have been required to develop their listening skills more effectively. Gloria Steinem (1983) has claimed that women's so-called "intuition" is a manifestation of their better developed listening skills. Some researchers, like sociologist Pamela Fishman (1983), claim that women have been socialized to engage in the emotional maintenance work of listening and attending to their conversational partners, while men are primarily taught to exchange information. These dichotomous expectations reflect a clear power imbalance. Of course, the individual expected to learn and anticipate the "meanings" of others, while her or his own messages are ignored, may come to resent the undue burden placed upon her or him. Fishman refers to this process as "interactional 'shitwork.'" Men who do not develop a sensitivity to their conversational partner's nuances and silences may regard the conversation as unfathomable and so miss out on important information.

When a man has been reared to regard his own message as paramount, he often interrupts other speakers and/or prepares his own response mentally while others are speaking rather than attending to the messages of others. In mixed-sex pairs, according to researchers Don H. Zimmerman and Candace West (1975), men overwhelmingly interrupt women and are more likely to unilaterally change the topic of conversation (West and Garcia, 1988).

He may not express his emotions. Another communication weakness that Warren Farrell (1972) ironically lists among the "Ten Commandments of Masculinity" is the dictum that because men "shalt not be vulnerable," they may not express "fear, weakness, sympathy, empathy or involvement" (cited in Duberman, 1975, p. 224). It may be a matter of individual men's own internalized homophobia or misogyny which leads them to restrain from emotional expressiveness—lest they be considered "effeminate." Also, because they are taught to value the logical, practical, and intellectual to the exclusion of the emotional, many men find it difficult to communicate emotions other than anger. Thus, in situations where men most desire intimacy and trust, the masculine dictum against expressing emotions may prove an enormous impediment. When one partner is routinely more self-disclosing and, therefore, more vulnerable, the result is a hierarchical rather than an egalitarian relationship.

He makes categorical assertions. The masculine stereotype encourages men to be authoritative and to make sweeping claims. This behavior appears to reflect self-assurance. However, by avoiding the communicative mode of qualification and indirection, often associated with "feminine" behavior, men may in fact be limited by their assertions. Carol Gilligan (1982) claims that the tendency to be more indirect and open to options can be an asset; this type of open communication is more than just a form of deference born of women's social subordination. As Gilligan states, "Sensitivity to the needs of others and the assumption of the responsibility for taking care lead women to attend to voices other than their own and to include in their judgement other points of view" (p. 16). When individuals sincerely desire open and honest communication among equals, they need to resist categorical assertions that reflect a preconceived mind set.

He dominates the discussion. A final aspect of the masculine stereotype is the assumption that men speak significantly less than women. In the gender-linked communication traits mentioned earlier, research has confirmed the fact that female and male behaviors do not generally reflect the respective stereotypes. However, numerous studies have shown that the assumption that men are less talkative than women is based on fiction rather than on fact (Argyle, Lalljee, and Cook, 1968; Strodtbeck and Mann, 1956). In mixed-sex groups, men routinely speak more than women and, in fact, usually dominate the conversations. Men are more likely to introduce the topics which are discussed, to interrupt others, and to initiate the changing of topics. Much of women's talk is devoted to drawing men into conversation and offering a number of topics from which males may choose (West, 1994).

The stereotype of the "strong, silent type" is a further example of potential domination integral to the masculine role. The silence of a more dominant partner does not necessarily denote listening. The withholding of speech can also imply power. Superiors need not answer subordinates, but subordinates are usually compelled to respond to superiors. In fact, the *refusal* to engage in conversation when another party clearly wants that engagement can be a form of conversational control. Equal "veto" power in a conversation is necessary for individuals to feel that they have established an effective communication climate. Therefore, any individual who dominates a discussion negatively influences the communication climate.

NONVERBAL ASPECTS OF THE STEREOTYPES

The "feminine" and "masculine" stereotypes that we have identified thus far have nonverbal components as well. Nonverbal behaviors imply a power differential and are associated with masculinity or femininity, regardless of who enacts them. Psychologist Nancy Henley (1977, p. 187) has identified gestures that communicate dominance and submission.

Dominance	*Submission*
Stare	Lower eyes, avert gaze, blink
Touch	Cuddle to the touch
Take up more space	Take up less than allotted space
Crowd another's space	Yield, move away
Frown, look stern	Smile
Point	Move in pointed direction; obey

It is largely through our nonverbal messages that we signal our gender identifications to others. We can observe that gestures of dominance are stereotypically associated with men, and those of submission are stereotypically associated with women. When power differences are communicated nonverbally, they are extremely difficult to isolate and to identify in context. As a result, much of how we picture gender appears innate rather than as a function of a pervasive, learned nonverbal communication behavior pattern.

In chapter 3, we will examine specific ways that masculinity and femininity are communicated nonverbally. At this point, it is important to note that cultural stereotypes for men and women, whether communicated through verbal or nonverbal channels, are as much symbols of power or powerlessness as they are models of gender differences.

In this chapter we have identified three important stereotypes: that of the "naturally" insecure, superficial, and weak woman; the "unnaturally" talkative, loud, and abrasive woman (both of these images are limiting); and the "confrontative," "logical" man of few words. We have also explored the negative implications of the masculine model of communication. For the most part, the feminine and masculine stereotypes represent traits that women and men, in given cultural settings at particular historical moments, have been reared to display. To that extent, they may be experienced as a social "fact." But since gender-linked traits are learned rather than innate behaviors, the stereotypes are also a "fiction."

The models of femininity and masculinity that many of us have internalized appear to have been with us for decades. Yet, as we have explained in the beginning of this chapter, linguistic practices—as sources of social power—have also been sources of resistance. Throughout history, there have been women and men who violated societal norms. Perhaps you have recognized in what ways you resist a wholesale enactment of the aforementioned stereotypes. However, resistance exacts a price; women have been labeled "unnatural" and "mannish" and men "effeminate" when they communicate in a manner which calls into question a strict and mutually exclusive gender dichotomy. At this point in time it has become apparent that a rigid adherence to the sex-role stereotypes is a disadvantage that limits both women and men, although in different ways. We believe that individuals are capable of creating other, less limiting communication models. In order to accomplish this, we first must examine in greater detail the specific verbal and nonverbal behaviors through which our respective stereotypes are manifested.

Suggested Activities

A. Focus on Listening: Vocal Stereotyping

1. Listen to a television soap opera with which you are unfamiliar. Turn off the picture and only listen to the voices. See if you can identify the "good," "bad," "sexy," "intelligent," and "dumb" character types by their vocal qualities.

   a. What are vocal characteristics of the "good" young wife? The debutante? The manipulator? What about the tough guy? The sincere, young lover?

   b. How is socioeconomic class indicated vocally?

   c. Do the characters' voices remind you of anyone you know? If so, do you have similar associations for both the character and your acquaintance because of how she or he sounds?

B. Focus on Interpersonal Communication and Vocal Stereotyping

1. Keep track of individuals to whom you speak who have noticeably different speech patterns from your own. Try to use their intonation pattern and mode of articulation when you converse. Note what happens.

   a. Is your partner aware of your adjustment?

   b. Does she or he think you sound "natural?"

   c. Is your partner more open and self-disclosing when you sound alike?

2. Tape a conversation between yourself and a speaker with a different native language. Listen to the pitch and intonation patterns; note the differences.

   a. What attitudes or character traits would these vocal behaviors connote for native-born North American English speakers?

   b. Have you assumed that your partner is shy, argumentative, elusive, or confrontative on the basis of an ethnocentric evaluation of vocal traits?

C. Focus on the Influence of Stereotyping

1. Ask a friend, a coworker, or a romantic partner to recall her/his initial impressions of you.

   a. What assumptions did he or she formulate and to what extent were these assumptions connected to specific verbal and nonverbal behaviors?

   b. Were these initial assumptions sustained; have they changed over time, and, if so, in what ways?

2. Either in groups or as part of a discussion, consider the extent to which the initial assumptions conformed to the masculine and feminine stereotypes addressed in this chapter and the extent to which these assumptions have changed over time.

Chapter Two

Vocal and Verbal Behaviors

[Woman] must have the skill to incline us to do everything which her sex will not enable her to do for herself . . . she should also have the art, by her own conversation, actions, looks and gestures, to communicate those sentiments which are agreeable to [men], without seeming to intend it.

— Jean Jacques Rousseau, *Emilius*

As Rousseau's quotation above illustrates, traditionally women and men have been taught to use language and nonverbal communication differently and for different purposes. (Did you just react with surprise when you read "women and men" instead of the more customary "men and women?" If so, you are starting to realize how ingrained habitual linguistic patterns become.)

When we published the first edition of this book in 1985, research supporting the existence of gender differences in communication was just coming to the attention of various disciplines. We recognize today that many of the differences observed in men's and women's communicative behavior were the result of *differences in relative power* between women and men in given situational contexts, *not essential attributes determined by female or male physiology*. In other words, the same speaker may act or speak in one way when communicating with his/her "significant other" and in another manner when interacting with her/his employee, supervisor, or student. Additionally, the attributes of the person being addressed, such as sex, culture, class, and relative degree of power, may be as salient as those of the speaker. While we, along with other recent theorists, recognize the importance for communication research of examining "some of the ways power and its expression (or repression) is gendered," we realize as well that in gender hierarchies, as in other cases of power inequities, subjugated groups can actively resist dominant codes (Longmire and Merrill, 1998, p. 1).

Therefore, while we examine differences and similarities in the verbal, vocal, and nonverbal strategies women and men have been found to adopt, it is always important to keep in mind a number of factors. For example, the *goal or intent of an interaction* may be different for different speakers. As we investigate some of the variables that comprise a communicative exchange, remember that communicators employ various *interactional strategies* depending on the context in which the interaction takes place and on their relationship with the person with whom they are communicating. Given the relative positions of women and men in a particular society, the strategies communicators adopt to achieve their various goals may vary by gender. As Kramarae (1981) noted, when women and men speak to each other, their intentions may be different. One's goal may be to build rapport while the other attempts to assert or resist control; one may communicate to maintain relationships or for the purpose of imposing one's will. And always bear in mind that differences *within* same-sex groups may be as significant as those found between women and men.

No one communicative behavior in isolation will give us a complete picture of similarities and differences in the ways men and women communicate. In this chapter we will investigate research on the ways women and men sound (paralinguistic or vocal messages), the linguistic choices (verbal messages) we make, and the interpretations or meanings that have been offered for these differences.

VOCAL BEHAVIORS

Articulation, or "How correct do you sound?"

Articulation comes from the Latin word for joint. It refers to the joining together of the organs of articulation (e.g., lips, tongue, teeth, glottis, etc.) so as to chop the breath stream into individual sounds. All speakers do not produce and pronounce speech sounds in the same way. For example, if one neglects to place his or her tongue tip between the upper and lower teeth in an attempt to produce a "th" sound (θ or ð), the result may sound like "t" or "d" as in the case of the speaker who says "dese tree tings" for "these three things."

Numerous studies have suggested that women in a given social setting are more likely to use standard phonetic and grammatical forms than are men. Males of similar socioeconomic groups are said to employ more casual and colloquial speech than are females. Shuy, Wolfram, and Riley's (1967) study of seven hundred Detroit residents demonstrated that men were more likely to nasalize the (Æ) vowel and drop "ing" endings in favor of the more casual "in'." For example: "The man was walkin' and talkin'." William Labov's (1972) studies in New York and Chicago, Peter Trudgill's (1975) research on British speakers in Norwich, England, and Walter Wolfram's (1969) studies of black English speakers in Detroit all indicate that women in each respective group used more standard forms than did men. Further research by Levine and Crockett (1979) on North Carolina speakers and Milroy (1980) on speakers from working-class communities in Belfast, Ireland, also found differences in women's and men's speech, with the women's articulation more closely approximating that of the standard or prestige dialect. In addition, both Levine's and Crockett and Milroy's studies determined that men's and women's pronunciation was most different from each other in working-class communities with dense social networks which may exert localized linguistic pressures on members of each group to sound as if they "belong"—to signal their identity through articulation. Beverly Hartford (1976) found that even when speaking English as a second language, native Spanish-speaking Chicanas (females) were more likely than Chicanos (males) to adopt the prestige forms of speech which are associated with middle-class native speakers and upward mobility.

However, before we uncritically accept these findings, let us examine some of the assumptions that undergird this research and the hypotheses which have been offered to account for the "gender difference" in how "correctly" speakers sound. First, since gender and socio-economic class are interconnected in these studies, it is important to call into question how the researchers above established the class membership of the women speakers they studied. Sociolinguist Deborah Cameron (1992) notes that most researchers merely assume that women are members of the same socioeconomic class as their husbands or fathers, therefore any "differences" observed are attributed to the speaker's gender. But individuals may well find partners in different socioeconomic classes or develop class identifications that differ from those of their parents. Further, educational and occupational differences may also account for the articulation differences researchers observed. For example, in Patricia Nichols's (1983) study of South

Carolina Gullah speakers (an African/English Creole dialect), she found the African-American women she researched far more likely to speak a standard dialect than their male family members. But Nichols also noted that the women she studied were largely employed in service occupations on the South Carolina mainland, while men were employed in other "blue collar" occupations. For women service workers, monolingual Gullah speaking would present an impediment when interacting with the (non-Gullah speaking) public, while the construction or agricultural jobs performed by men of the same community did not require a similar degree of communication with outsiders.

Beth Thomas's (1989) study of Welsh speakers, however, found that, contrary to the studies cited above, the speech of women she researched was less standard than that of men in their community. Thomas examined older, nonworking women whose speech preserved a nonstandard vernacular feature that the speech of men in the same community did not. Thomas attributed the difference between women's and men's speech, and the women's more colloquial usage, to their active participation in local chapels which reinforced their speech solidarity.

Given these apparently contradictory findings how do we account for gender differences in articulation? Trudgill (1975) offered two explanations for the fact that the women and men he studied appeared to employ different degrees of standard articulation. He believed that because women within any given social strata are generally regarded as subordinate to men, they find the need to "secure and signal their status linguistically" (p. 91) through more standard speech. Second, since less formal, more working-class pronunciation is often associated with toughness and masculinity, women are frequently encouraged to differentiate themselves from such associations—to talk like "ladies."

Having taught and lived in working-class environments, it has been our experience that many males have been raised to associate working-class speech with toughness and virility and to believe that studying and "improving" one's articulation is an effeminate undertaking. But working-class women's use of or aspirations toward more formal speech need not be a result of either their status consciousness or their desire to present themselves as more "feminine." We can all observe the pervasive ridicule of working-class women's voices in popular culture. For example, television depictions of characters like "Roseanne" and "The Nanny" cast women with working-class dialects as objects of derision—unintelligent, and frequently irritating, for all their street-smart toughness. Women are largely judged by their appearance, and speech strongly affects how they appear to others.

For all the prescriptive force of stereotypes about how women and men *should* sound, it is necessary to look very carefully at the conditions of particular communities, at what the members themselves consider to be the most salient influences on their behavior, and at what they are using their speech to "announce" about themselves. Articulation is a strong indicator of in-group belonging, and our group memberships, including those in same-sex groups, are multiple and complex.

Pitch, or "How big do you sound?"

A fundamental difference in the way that women and men sound is that women's voices are generally higher pitched than men's. It is partially the size of one's vocal tract that determines pitch. A large person would be expected to have longer, thicker vocal cords and therefore would speak with a lower pitch. A small person with shorter, thinner vocal cords would be expected to have a higher pitched voice. However, individuals may change their pitch by changing the position of their lips when producing vowel sounds. More open lips shorten the vocal tract and thus raise the pitch. For example, people who speak while smiling produce higher pitched sounds than those who do not.

Over the past several years, numerous female students who have registered for our classes in Gender, Conflict Management, and Intercultural Communication, bemoaned the fact that "nature" had saddled them with squeaky, high-pitched, "little girl" voices. However, studies by Ignatius Mattingly (1966) and Jacqueline Sachs, Philip Lieberman and Donna Erickson (1973) indicate that the observed differences in pitch between males and females are much greater than anatomy logically could explain. In his studies of men, women, and child speakers, Mattingly found that male and female speakers of the same dialect tended to form vowels differently, thereby affecting their pitch. Mattingly concluded that the pitch differences were largely the result of social and linguistic conventions rather than purely the result of physiological differences. Similarly, when listening to the recorded voices of preadolescent children with larynxes of the same size relative to their weight, adult judges were able to identify the sex of the children solely by listening to tapes. These researchers have hypothesized that, regardless of the size of the larynx and vocal cords, males and females may be adjusting their pitch to fit cultural expectations and stereotypes. This adjustment can be heard as well in bilingual speakers who alter their pitch with the language they are speaking.

Although researchers do not discount the fact that hormonal differences may account for some variation, they speculate that by adjusting the way sounds are produced, *males tend to make themselves sound as though they are larger and females as though they are smaller* than the articulatory mechanism alone would suggest. (Later in this book we will discuss the extent to which size communicates power nonverbally.) Thus, women who have adopted excessively high-pitched voices may sound giddy and childish, and they are frequently not taken seriously. Yet the fact is, to some extent, pitch is a learned feature of one's speech.

Erving Goffman (1977) has examined the ways men and women are taught to display gender. Goffman contends that the verbal and nonverbal interactions between women and men have *produced* differences that are attributed to gender. Goffman describes numerous interactions—from bear hugs to threats via pushes or other forms of "teasing"—whereby males encourage females "to provide a full-voiced rendition of the plight to which her sex is presumably prone" (p. 323). Thus, a female's assumption of a higher than natural pitch may be a behavior learned and reinforced in a multitude of interactions throughout her life. Social prescriptions about gender and pitch are frequently reinforced by speech pathologists who work with transsexual clients and endeavor to teach them to raise or lower their pitch to suit the expectations of their new sex and gender identity.

As a rule, in the United States lower-pitched voices seem to be regarded more positively by both women and men. In fact, William Austin (1965) found that the act of *imitating a person of either sex* with a derogatory, high-pitched feminine voice was perceived as an infuriating "act of aggression." Since an artificially high pitch can be associated with timidity, childishness and/or weakness, it is not surprising that most individuals would be insulted to be depicted in this fashion.

Stereotypes about the sound of women's voices have been offered as an excuse for occupational prejudices. In the early decades of the twentieth century the technology of both telephonic and radio communication developed. Interestingly, from the outset, women were employed as telephone operators, on the pretext that their voices would sound "pleasing" and broadcast well over phone wires, but these same "pleasing" voices were considered unsuitable for radio broadcasts. Obviously, it was not a matter of a speaker's pitch, but the difference in socially ascribed power and prestige that deemed women's voices appropriate for giving information in the service career of phone operator but restricted women from the higher-status occupation of radio announcer (Martin, 1972). For many years women in the United States were denied access to careers in broadcasting on the pretext that the higher-pitched female voice did not sound serious enough, although in France the female voice has been *preferred* for news broadcasting. The voices of women who are employed in the broadcast media tend to be lower-pitched than those of the female population at large. We have progressed considerably from the time when the only female voices on the nightly television news were those of the "cute" (i.e., not serious) "weather girls." Interestingly enough, when broadcast weather predictions became more scientific, the weather "girl" was replaced by a male meteorologist. Many people still tend to regard a lower-pitched man's voice as the voice of authority. Overwhelmingly, men's voices are used in advertising voiceovers, even in ads for household products that are purchased and used almost exclusively by women.

What, then, are the implications for women whose natural voices are somewhat higher than those of men? First, women need to be aware of whether they are fulfilling a stereotype by employing an even higher pitch than necessary. If so, they must examine the settings in which they are most likely to use this voice. Does this occur most frequently with friends, lovers, parents, or employers? Is it a subconscious strategy a speaker adopts when she fears that her message might threaten the person with whom she speaks? It may be that women adopt this particular guise of powerlessness when they anticipate resentment of their strength. If so, speakers can practice exercises to lower their pitch. (See the suggested activities at the end of the chapter.) Second, we might reconsider the cause and effect association many intuit between higher-pitched women's voices and childishness. Are women's voices devalued because they really do sound childlike, or, are higher pitches devalued because they are associated with women? Third, all of us need to guard against judging individuals as if their pitch were a barometer of their capabilities, intelligence, or maturity.

Intonation, or "How certain do you sound?"

Related to pitch is intonation. While pitch refers to the general high or low quality of the voice, intonation refers to the pitch swings or changes within a phrase or sentence. Every language has its own intonation patterns. North American English speakers usually employ a rising intonation for most questions (except those preceded by inter-rogative words, e.g., *who, what, when, where, why,* and *how*), to express hesitancy or uncertainty, and to indicate incompleteness of a thought (as in listing items in a series). A falling intonation is used to give commands, state facts, and to ask questions that begin with inter-rogative words.

Linguist Sally McConnell-Ginet (1983) has hypothesized that the basic intonational system of a language may be used differently by women than by men. Women English speakers are more likely than men to employ intonational patterns that feature upward inflections and a wider range of pitches that change frequently. Ruth Brend's (1975) studies found that most men used only three levels of intonation contrasts, while a majority of women used four. Men tend to avoid final patterns that do not end at their lowest pitch level. For example, a woman professional is much more likely to invite someone into her office with an upward inflected "Come in?" Her male colleague's "Come in" with a downward glide may sound more like a command than a polite invitation.

North American male English speakers appear to avoid those intonational patterns which have been stigmatized as feminine, except in an intentional deviation from stereotyped behavior in order to present oneself as "gay" or in a hostile imitation of women (Austin 1965; Terango 1966). In fact, Terango found that the greater variety of pitches a speaker used, coupled with the rapidity of the change from one pitch to another, was a more salient marker of "feminine" speech than the overall highness of the speaker's pitch. However, nationality and dialect as well as gender influence pitch patterns. British, Irish, or Caribbean English speakers, and speakers of other languages employ-ing the intonation pattern associated with their native usage, do not adhere to the specific gendered pitch patterns described here. How-ever, because their speech marks them as "foreign," listeners are less likely to perceive them as deviating from gender stereotypes.

Robin Lakoff (1975) described North American women's "charac-teristic" intonation patterns as reflective of hesitancy, uncertainty, or lack of assertiveness. Lakoff claimed that when offering a declarative answer to a question, women often use a rising pattern, which sounded to her as though they were asking for confirmation, approval, or doubt-ing their own answer. For example, in response to the question, "When are you free to meet with me?", women speakers were more likely to reply "In about . . . twenty minutes . . . ?" with an upward inflection. A response of "In twenty minutes" with a downward pattern would sound decisive and definitive, Lakoff felt, and might imply that the addressee had no choice but to wait. The latter intonation pattern would support a superior or equal rather than a subordinate position. Other researchers interpret the stereotypically "feminine" rising pitch pattern not as a weakness of women's speech, but as a polite form in that it conveys to listeners a speaker who is leaving a decision open, rather than imposing his/her will upon an addressee.

Subsequent researchers have called into question such bipolar interpretations of intonation patterns. Carole Edelsky (1979) found that *the person addressed by a speaker* contributed to the intonation the speaker used. In Edelsky's study, women responding to a question about which they were certain were more likely to employ a rising-falling-rising intonation when speaking with another woman than with a male interviewer. Edelsky interpreted her subjects' rising intonation as an auditory marker of openness, signifying a desire for a longer exchange, rather than a reflection of a speaker's insecurity. Similarly, Barrie Thorne noted the extensive use of the high rising intonation among feminists speaking with one another. Thorne attributed this style to "an invitation to others to speak, emphasizing the collectivity of the group and underscoring a speaker's desire not to present herself as a 'heavy'" (quoted in McConnell-Ginet, 1983, p. 85).

A third interpretation of the high rising upward swing such as in a speaker's utterance of "In . . . twenty minutes . . .?" is that the rising intonation may be reflective of a further implied but unarticulated question. Questions, such as "Is twenty minutes alright for your schedule?" or "Do you think twenty minutes will leave us enough time to complete our business?", or incompletely articulated thoughts, such as "I am busy at this moment. I estimate the work will take twenty minutes to complete, but it may take longer," may be communicated paralinguistically by the upward swing in intonation (McConnell-Ginet, 1983; Ladd, 1980).

Earlier researchers, following Lakoff, were quick to label the upward swing and frequent and rapid pitch changes which are said to characterize "feminine" delivery as markers of insecurity, incompleteness, hesitancy, or doubt. The more monotone delivery associated with men's speech was viewed as a norm against which women's more expressive voices sounded excessive. Just as we need to resist accepting the stereotypes that define certain pitch patterns as indicative of "hysteria" or "whining," we should resist characterizing lack of vocal variety as a sign of "keeping one's cool" or emotional detachment.

We must become cognizant of the extent to which vocal behavior is interpreted as a signal of the speaker's attitude about him- or herself and toward the listener. We need also be aware that in different languages and dialects, pitch, intonation patterns, and a range of standards of articulation carry different connotations. The instructor who encourages nonnative students merely to imitate her or his pitch and intonation patterns, without explaining the social connotations of these patterns, may be compounding rather than alleviating problems. In our attitudes about men and women, whatever their native language or dialect, we need to be careful to separate what we have heard from what we assume the speaker meant to say. Yet, because so much of the "meaning" of our messages is communicated paralinguistically, listeners often "read" attitudes, such as sarcasm, condescension, or uncertainty, and personality qualities, such as insensitivity or insecurity, into the sound of our voices. The vocal qualities of our speech combine with the words we use to shape others' interpretations of us.

VERBAL CONSTRUCTS

For several decades, researchers have been attempting to determine whether the words speakers use and the way they arrange their utterances syntactically are related to the speaker's gender. Sociolinguists have much evidence to suggest that geographic region, socioeconomic factors, educational level, and ethnic identification all influence the dialects we speak and the vocabulary we draw upon. In the 1970s, researchers such as Lakoff (1975), Kramer (1974), and Thorne and Henley (1975) proposed the possibility that women—as a result of their relatively subordinate social position—were discouraged from using "powerful" language and so may speak a "women's language" or "genderlect" that is characterized by the usage of certain vocabulary, qualifiers, disclaimers, tag questions, and compound requests.

In the first edition of this book (1985) we reported those findings uncritically. However, subsequent research has pointed to new and more complex approaches to and explanations for the gender differences reported in some of the earlier findings. As we mentioned above, there is now greater awareness of the fact that conversational strategies are coconstructed; that is, the person with whom one is communicating and the situational context influence a speaker's verbal strategies. Speech, in both its vocal and verbal dimensions, is a marker of in-group solidarity. Part of the metacommunicative message that runs through many verbal exchanges is an attempt at an unconscious matching, as if one were saying "See, we speak the same 'language'; we can understand each other." So, a speaker may elect one set of verbal constructs in a personal or professional situation with equal status conversational partners and employ an entirely different strategy when communicating with a person over whom she or he has authority or to whom she or he shows deference. Furthermore, there is less homogeneity among women and men than was previously assumed. Just because women or men of *a particular group* communicated in a particular manner in a given research study, we cannot assume their behavior is representative of *all women* or *all men*. As you read about the following verbal constructs, examine your own behavior. How do you signal your "identity" verbally? Do you employ different strategies with same- or opposite-sex friends? With members of your own or different cultural groups? With elder family members? In the classroom? In the workplace?

Qualifiers, or "I sort of think maybe you know what I mean," and Intensifiers, or "I'm sooo very, very glad to hear it"

The use of qualifiers (such as "sort of," "kind of," "rather," "really," "I think," "I guess") has been found by some researchers to be more common in the speech of women than in men. Crosby and Nyquist (1977) determined that role relationships influenced the use of qualifiers and, in their studies, women more than men qualified their messages. A qualifier softens the statement in which it appears. "I am *sort of* disappointed in your work this quarter" sounds less critical to a listener than an unqualified statement. Even the words "actually" and "really," or "very" and "so" which may appear at first glance to intensify an expression, do, in fact, soften it. "I *really* don't want to be disturbed" is less assertive than "I don't want to be disturbed." The need for "actually" and "really" may imply that the speaker believes that she or he will not be taken seriously without the added emphasis.

When speakers qualify their statements, they sound less categorical and are less likely to offend listeners. Some researchers, like William O'Barr and Bowman Atkins (1980), have analyzed the use of qualifiers, intensifiers, tag questions, and disclaimers (discussed in the next section) in courtroom settings. O'Barr and Atkins contend that use of these constructs is indicative of a speaker's relative lower status—a subordinate speaker communicating with more powerful listeners—and is thus more related to factors like socioeconomic class and educational experience than to gender. O'Barr and Atkins found in their study of courtroom testimony that lower-status men used the verbal constructs assumed by some to mark "women's speech," while higher-status women avoided them. However, it is not merely the fact that speakers use a given construct that concerns us, rather it is the types of meanings that listeners assign to this usage. Patricia Bradley (1981) found that the use of qualifiers was only perceived negatively if *the speaker was a woman*. When men used qualifiers in their speech, they were perceived as being considerate and polite, rather than weak and unassertive. It may be that persons already presumed to be in a dominant position are regarded positively whenever they signal a willingness to mitigate their power.

Newcombe and Arnkoff (1979) found that qualifiers may be appropriate when we want to convey warmth, politeness, or caring. However, if they are employed routinely—as a hedge against taking a verbal stand—these "crutches" may get in the way. As we examine some of the meanings associated with these verbal constructs and those discussed below, the gender of the speaker and of the listener are only two of many variables to keep in mind.

Disclaimers, or "This probably doesn't mean anything, but . . ."

Disclaimers are excuses or apologies offered by a speaker before she or he makes a remark. Several studies conducted between the 1970s and 1990s reported that women were more likely than men to use such disclaimers as "This probably isn't important, but . . ." or "I'm not really sure about this, however . . ." in interactions with both same- and mixed-sex conversational partners (Carli, 1990; Eakins and Eakins, 1978; Grob and Allen, 1996; Stutman, 1987). By using these expressions, speakers, in effect, distance themselves from their claims rather than stand behind them. The disclaimer may serve, in part, as an apology for speaking. It can also signal an audience not to associate the speaker too closely with her or his message—not to take the speaker "seriously." This defensive device may reassure a speaker that her or his message can be rejected without the speaker being rejected. When individuals use disclaimers, their message is minimized before it is uttered. The disclaimer may lead listeners to believe that the speaker lacks knowledge, is unprepared, or lacks strong conviction. Disclaimers convey the impression that the speaker has to apologize in advance to gain the goodwill of an audience who may otherwise not be receptive.

In our work with female students and with nonnative English speakers of both sexes (who often preface remarks to monolingual English speakers with apologies that "my English isn't so good"), we have encouraged them to examine their use of disclaimers. Disclaimers may be used as part of a strategy to ingratiate oneself to a possibly prejudiced or inattentive audience. Listeners need to be aware that their responses to speakers may be encouraging the use of disclaimers; listeners bear a responsibility to demonstrate verbally and nonverbally that they are attentive and receptive to the speaker. When speakers are made to feel that they are being listened to willingly, they will be less likely to punctuate their remarks with disclaimers. While we encourage women speakers to abandon any self-effacing strategy, we recommend that listeners ask themselves, "What have I done or am I doing to make this speaker feel that she or he has my attention?"

Tag Questions, or "This is what I meant, isn't it?"

A tag question is an expression midway between an outright statement and a yes/no question. An example of a tag question is "We have an appointment at three o'clock, don't we?" The tag "don't we?" is an attempt to gain confirmation from one's listener. Robin Lakoff (1975) has asserted that women use this construction more frequently than do men and that its use is a marker of insecurity. Lakoff felt that a speaker using a tag question was avoiding committing him/herself to an outright statement while trying to hedge against one of the possible responses to a bipolar (yes/no) question. If the speaker asks "Do we have an appointment at three o'clock?" she or he risks equally the possibilities of receiving a negative or affirmative response. The tag question is also, therefore, a leading question in that the respondent is led in a particular direction. Tag questions have also been seen as approval seeking for either the speaker or the speaker's message.

Studies of the usage of tag questions have yielded complex and contradictory findings. In support of Lakoff's contention that tag questions are a common feature in women's speech, several researchers conducted studies where women were found to use more tag questions than were men (Beck, 1988; Carli, 1990; Fishman, 1980; Holmes, 1984; Lesch, 1994). These findings, moreover, emerged in a range of settings in both personal and professional contexts, in same-sex as well as mixed-sex interactions, and in dyads (interactions between two people) as well as in small groups. But other researchers, such as Dubois and Crouch (1975) and Johnson (1980) conducted studies in professional contexts where men were found to use more tag questions than did their female colleagues, and Deborah Cameron, Fiona McAlinden, and Kathy O'Leary (1989) found men and women subjects employing a roughly equal amount of tags. How do we account for these discrepancies, and how do we determine what tag questions "mean" to listeners?

Researchers offer a variety of divergent interpretations for the tag question construct. While some contend that a tag question reflects a woman speaker's subordinate status or uncertainty, an alternate interpretation is that women employ tag questions primarily as a means of affiliation—with the tag functioning as a means to elicit responses, to sustain interaction, or to invite discussion with conversational partners (Beck, 1988; Carli, 1990; Fishman, 1980; Holmes, 1984; Lesch, 1994). For example, Pamela Fishman (1980) claimed that women in the heterosexual couples she studied performed more of the verbal interaction work in maintaining their relationships and therefore used tags to engage their partners in dialogue, not to convey uncertainty. Johnson (1980) also found that the use of tags, which request responses from listeners, helped sustain conversations. The tag, such as the French "*n'est-ce pas*?" or the Spanish "*¿Es verdad*?", may be an attempt to keep the conversational ball rolling by engaging the listener. Lakoff also noted the role tag questions play in small talk; there are few icebreakers in the entry-acquaintance phase of a relationship that are more innocuous than "It's a nice day, isn't it?" Thus, in some cases the use of tag questions may be a polite attempt to engage in nonthreatening conversation.

In contrast, other researchers who have attributed men's use of tag questions to an attempt *to gain confirmation* for their statements, rather than approval, see this verbal behavior as indicative of an instrumental rather than an affiliative response to conversational partners (Beck, 1988; Holmes, 1984; Maltz and Borker, 1982). Arliss (1991), Borisoff and Merrill (1991), and Dubois and Crouch (1975) all observe that tag questions also may be used in an intimidating or overbearing way to assure a response which negates the listener's possibility of opposition. Depending on the intonation, it may be condescending to ask "You won't do that again, will you?" or "I told you to finish this report by Thursday, didn't I?" Tag questions, like all linguistic constructs, must be understood within the specific contexts in which they are uttered, including the relative degrees of dominance experienced by all parties. Because the tag form can be used to convey various connotations, from uncertainty to politeness to a genuine question to intimidation, it is neither inherently "weak" nor "strong" as earlier researchers claimed. As the research on tag questions demonstrates, it is impossible to consider vocal and verbal behaviors in isolation; whatever meaning is associated with a tag question is determined by the question in concert with a given delivery style.

Compound Requests, or "How many words shall I use to make my wishes known?"

Despite stereotypes to the contrary, women often have more difficulty voicing requests and demands than men. Individuals who are accustomed to wielding considerable personal power are more likely to use imperatives than are subordinates. For example, "Type this now!" is a command issued by a speaker who assumes that his or her authority is such that the addressee is compelled to comply. On the other hand, "Can you type this now?" is an indirect request in the form of an inquiry (i.e.: "Are you available to type this now?" versus "Please type this now.") Lakoff maintained that women were more likely than men to compound their requests. The more a request is compounded, the more polite it sounds, because the listener has increasingly greater latitude to refuse. The most indirect request, "If it's not too much trouble, would you please type this now?" is worded negatively to imply the greater possibility of the addressee's refusal.

Speakers and listeners of both sexes should be aware of how they choose to phrase their requests to others. Those who routinely employ indirect compound forms may find that, on occasion, a more direct, less apologetic tone is more expedient. However, speakers who characteristically use imperatives need to take responsibility for how they phrase their messages as well as for what they say. Many male speakers, in particular, are baffled when their listeners bridle at being *ordered* to do something that the speaker *intended* as a *request* rather than as a command. Both strategies—direct and polite—are necessary skills to master, although as we explain in chapter 5, markers of common courtesy, such as "please" and "thank you," result in more positive evaluations of communicators.

Vocabulary Differences, or "Which words are whose?"

French psychoanalyst Luce Irigaray (1987) has found in her experimental work that the women and men she has studied use language differently. For example, Irigaray found men far more likely than women to begin sentences with the first person pronoun *je* (I) and so to make themselves the active subjects of written and spoken discourse. Irigaray sees such differences in usage as evidence of women's effacement in language and as an indicator of a speaker's subjective sense of self.

Researchers studying English speakers find certain words and categories of words appear more frequently in the speech of women in a range of given social, economic, and geographical contexts than in the speech of men. Adverbs of intensity (such as awfully, terribly, pretty, quite, so) and some adjectives (such as charming, lovely, adorable, dreadful, ghastly, divine) appear more commonly used by white, middle-class, North American English speaking women than by men. We do not observe this same distinction in the lexicon of male and female British English speakers, however. Steckler and Cooper (1980) also found that North American women employed more specific color terms than did men. Specific words for colors like taupe, mauve, puce, lavender, and violet are not common in men's speech. Men are more likely to use combination terms, such as "reddish brown" rather than "rust." In order to understand why speakers use or avoid particular words, we need to explore what the usage of specific terms is seen to signify about a speaker.

Some theorists contend that the usage of specific terms for gradations and nuances of color leads listeners to regard speakers as trivial and superficial because of the attention paid to subtle distinctions and details. Others associate this lexical difference to traditional sex-role socialization. Because decoration of self and environment have been traditionally assumed to be a concern of women, specific terms for colors may be more familiar to women. However, this does not explain why men avoid using these terms, particularly since we could argue that the ability to discern and to describe more subtle differences in color is a strength, not a detriment, and a matter of perception available equally to men and women. Men may resist discussing the "lovely mauve drapes" in the conference room or the "streaks of lavender" in the sunset as a result of internalized homophobia, since when men do use words that are stereotypically part of the female lexicon, they risk being considered effeminate. It appears that the association with femininity has tainted the terms and not any quality inherent in the lexicon of terms for color.

Conversely, forceful expletives like damn and hell have long been considered much more acceptable in middle-class men's speech than in women's. In fact, in some quarters, men have been taught to apologize if they inadvertently "curse" in a woman's presence, as though the mere exposure to "curses" or strong expletives were potentially damaging to women. Women risk being regarded as unfeminine when they use these words, particularly in mixed-sex groups. Instead, women have been encouraged that it is more polite to use such expressions as "dear me," "oh my," and "goodness." These particles are less forceful than those allowed men, and their use tends to weaken or to render trivial the expression that follows them. For example, it would sound ludicrous for an executive of either sex to say, "Dear me, you mean we lost the multimillion dollar contract?" or for an attorney to remark, "Oh, goodness. I hope we don't have another hung jury."

Increasingly, women in many social groups are more likely to employ expletives more common in men's speech to convey strong emotions. Men rarely, however, use "women's" particles. As we mentioned above, men may fear being stigmatized for their use of "feminine" words, whereas women who display their mastery of the vocabulary and behaviors more frequently associated with men are not demeaned for their verbal demonstration of this knowledge. As Lakoff explains, "The language of the favored group, the group that holds power . . . is generally adopted by the other group, and not vice versa" (1975, p. 10). As we consider the verbal behaviors of men and women, we need to bear in mind how gender stereotypes and stigmas are related to language use and avoidance.

VERBAL AND VOCAL BEHAVIORS IN INTERACTION

Thus far, we have been discussing particular vocal and verbal behaviors, but communication is more than isolated behaviors; it is a dynamic exchange between two or more people in a given relational context. We will now explore the behaviors that occur in interactions between speakers.

Dyadic communication refers to communication between two individuals. Men and women are engaged in same- and mixed-sex dyads as friends, lovers, spouses, colleagues, employers and employees, clinicians and patients, teachers and students, and so forth. (In chapter 5 we discuss the specific applications of dyadic communication in professional settings.) One person speaks; another listens, comments on what she or he has heard, and offers a message which is, in turn, heard and responded to by the first speaker. A simple conversation? Perhaps. However, often a gendered hierarchy of power is established and maintained as an implicit feature in the interaction. In mixed-sex dyads who talks more? Is gender a variable in same-sex interactions as well? By what tactics (such as interruption or refusal to discuss a topic offered) does one speaker seize control of a conversation, gain the "floor," negotiate for speaker turn-taking, and affirm or disconfirm the contributions of her/his conversational partner? Much of the research findings cited below come from mixed-sex studies where interactions between men and women subjects were investigated and compared. We still know far too little about the interactions of same-sex couples or groups and how questions of relative power, dominance, or affiliation inform those interactions.

Talk Time

Contrary to stereotypes, much research on communication interactions in settings and relationships as diverse as the laboratory, the home, among married couples (Kenkel, 1963; Fishman, 1983), colleagues, students (Duncan and Fiske, 1977), complete strangers (Marlatt, 1970), university faculty meetings (Eakins and Eakins, 1978), professional conferences (Swacker, 1976) and jury deliberations (Strodtbeck, James, and Hawkins, 1957; Strodtbeck and Mann, 1956) indicates that men talk for longer amounts of time than the women with whom they interact. Some researchers, like Fred Strodtbeck and his colleagues (in their studies on jury deliberation), found power and status variables as well; men and/or persons of higher status hold the floor for a longer time than women and/or persons of lower status. Even when expertise is taken into consideration, Leet-Pellegrini (1980) found that male experts talked more than female experts.

How do we account for the popular perception that women talk more than men? Dale Spender (1980) has claimed that the stereotype of women's talkativeness, despite all evidence to the contrary, comes from an error in comparison. "Women have not been judged on the basis of whether they talk more than men, but of whether they talk more than silent women" (p. 42). Spender feels that silence is the desired state for women in a patriarchal order where speech equals power, and so "any talk in which a woman engages" is liable to be considered "too much" (p. 42). Furthermore, much of women's talk, according to linguist Julia Penelope (1990), is an attempt either to ward off interruption or to encourage a response from a conversational partner, as we will see below.

Topic Initiation and Topic Selection

Numerous studies have established that in mixed-sex dyads women work harder than men at asking questions and attempting to initiate topics (Fishman, 1983; West, 1994). In many dyads, or in mixed-sex small groups, women have a hard time getting the floor or getting topics of their choosing discussed. Women and other persons in subordinate positions may offer and attempt to initiate numerous different topics, but the person in a more dominant position frequently selects the topics actually discussed by ignoring some conversational overtures and responding to others. Some researchers define *topic initiation* to include the mere mentioning of a new topic; others refer to the successful selection of that topic by all conversational partners. Thus, the data in this area may at first appear contradictory (Aries, 1976, 1982; West, 1994). As Fishman (1983, p. 91) notes:

> In a sense, every remark or turn at speaking should be seen as an attempt to interact. It may be an attempt to open or close a conversation. It may be a bid to continue interaction, to respond to what went before, and elicit a further remark from one's partner. Some attempts succeed; others fail. For an attempt to succeed, the other party must be willing to do further interactional work. That other person has the power to turn an attempt into a conversation or to stop it dead.

Fishman notes that women use questions to gain attention and ensure a response from their conversational partners. Fishman found that women were also more likely than men to preface their remarks with the statement "This is interesting. . . ." These expressions may reflect a speaker's perceived need to gain the attention of a listener by provoking interest or attesting to the worthiness of the remark to follow—attention the speaker might not otherwise secure. In numerous studies, women offered more conversational openings than did men; however, fewer of the topics women attempted to initiate were actually selected.

Candace West (1994) has explored the mechanisms by which conversational partners arrive at, shift, and terminate topics. In her recent research using conversational analysis methodology, she found men more likely than women to engage in unilateral topic transitions. In addition, West investigated and interpreted a particular form of silence or inactivity, one person's "refraining from asking [a question of the other] when it was clear that the other badly want[ed] to be asked" (p. 378). This impervious response she found more prevalent in men than in women studied. More dominant partners can control and dominate the topic and direction of conversation by their choice to ignore as well as to participate in a discussion.

An interesting study by Courtright, Millar, and Rogers-Millar (1979) relates the degree of domineeringness of marital partners with the tendency on the part of the less dominant spouse to ask more questions rather than to offer assertions and opinions. Courtright and his colleagues found that the more dominant the husband, when compared with the wife, the more questions asked by the wife. However, in the case of more dominant wives, husbands did not necessarily ask more questions.

Self-Disclosure

The ability to reveal information about ourselves or our feelings that is not readily known to others has been regarded consistently as an essential characteristic of both romantic and platonic intimate relationships. However, much has been written to suggest that both early socialization and cultural norms inhibit men's expression of feelings and emotions other than anger (Bem, 1993; Borisoff, 1993; Gilligan, 1982; Haste, 1994; Hatfield and Rapson, 1993; Keen, 1991; Levant, 1996; Rubin, 1983; Wood and Inman, 1993). These studies have led writers such as Hatfield and Rapson to suggest that men "fail to take [intimacy] seriously enough to learn about it or develop techniques to aid in gaining a measure of it" (p. 133); that men choose to talk about "facts" rather than feelings (Maltz and Borker, 1982; Rubin 1983; Tannen, 1990); that men "focus their conversations more on sports, work, or issues external to the individual" (Aries, 1987, pp. 162–63); and that, as a result, heterosexual men's same-sex friendships are less intimate and rewarding than friendships between women (Reisman, 1990; Williams, 1985).

Several researchers attribute reputed differences in men's and women's self-disclosure to gender socialization, suggesting that women and men have been taught to express closeness and vulnerability in different contexts: for women, closeness may emerge from self-disclosure in dyadic interaction; for men, feelings of closeness may be more likely to develop from shared activities, rather than as a verbal exchange of personal information situated within dyadic interaction (Borisoff and Hahn, 1995a; Duck, 1988, 1991; Rubin, 1983; Swain, 1989; Wood and Inman, 1993). In their respective works on male-male bonding and female-female bonding, both Chris Inman (1996) and Fern Johnson (1996) conclude that mutual caring, understanding, trust, loyalty, enjoyment, and the need to connect are characteristic of same-sex friendships. While these may emerge from sharing activities as well as sharing dialogue, self-disclosure demands—in Rubin's terms—"some willingness to allow another into our inner life, into the thoughts and feelings that live there" (Rubin 1985, p. 74).

Some recent studies raise questions about the existence and "meanings" of gender differences in self-disclosure. Dindia and Allen (1992) have directly challenged other researchers' claims about differences in men's and women's disclosures. Their meta-analysis of 205 empirical studies spanning a thirty-year period found few actual differences, leading them to conclude that "it is time to stop perpetuating the myth that there are large sex differences in men's and women's self-disclosure" (p. 118). As always, we need to be wary of totalizing notions of "men's" and "women's" behaviors which erase differences within those groups. For example, Gaines (1995) found that African-American men tended to be more emotionally expressive than were men of Caucasian backgrounds, suggesting that the "differences" between women and men reported above may reflect more complex constructions of ethnicity and other variables, such as sexuality, as well as gender.

Moreover, as Timothy Edgar (1994) has recently established, "although hundreds of studies of self-disclosure have been published, there has been no systematic effort to analyze *the content of 'real life' disclosive messages*" (p. 224). Since the information one discloses may have the potential to discredit or stigmatize individual communicators, self-disclosure may signify *vulnerability* as well as *intimacy*. Thus, connections between an individual's gender and her or his strategic practice—or avoidance—of disclosing need to be examined carefully so as not merely to perpetuate or reify the masculine stereotype discussed in the previous chapter.

The person with whom one communicates, as well as the interactional context, appear to be salient features in self-disclosure. In his study of gay men's disclosure of their sexual orientation, Edgar (1994) discovered that disclosures that are highly sensitive and potentially stigmatizing were "strategically formulated and enacted" and that *the recipient of the message* played a vital role in the formulation and timing of the speaker's disclosure (p. 233–34). In fact, sociologist Lillian Rubin found men more likely to disclose emotionally charged personal information to women who were relative strangers than to men they defined as intimate friends. Yet in her extensive study of men's and women's friendships, Rubin noted "an inchoate wish" on the part of the men she interviewed "to relax the . . . internal constraints that kept these men from giving expression to their feelings" (Rubin, 1985, p. 72), particularly their feelings of closeness to other men. Rubin attributes the resistance many heterosexual men experience to expressing their emotional attachment to other men to internalized homophobia, a concern she claims is less prevalent in women's same-sex relationships (p. 100–101).

Although a comprehensive examination of gender and self-disclosure is beyond the purview of this text, it is clear that divergent perceptions of ways men and women develop and express closeness and vulnerability in the relationships they forge merit further scrutiny. We recognize that a society's prescriptions for femininity and masculinity inevitably inform how individuals initially learn to enact verbal demonstrations of intimacy or vulnerability. As with all the verbal interactions explored in this chapter, the setting, the relationship between conversational partners, the actual "motives, intentions, and expectations of the communicators" (Aries, 1987, p. 170), along with the respective gender, ethnicity, sexuality, and socioeconomic class of each, may contribute to the degree and kind of self-disclosing, as well as to the "meanings" attributed to it.

Interruptions and Overlaps

One of the most debated interaction patterns is the interruption. Interrupting another individual before he or she has finished speaking is a clear sign, according to Ralph Nichols (1948), of ineffective listening. Speakers who are interrupted frequently feel dominated, disregarded, or muted by the interjection of another speaker before they have finished their "conversational turn."

The majority of studies conducted between the 1970s and the 1990s all found evidence that in mixed-sex conversations between couples, colleagues, and adult strangers, men overwhelmingly interrupt women (Carli, 1990; Eakins and Eakins, 1978; Mulac et al., 1988;

Leet-Pellegrini, 1980; Turner, Dindia, and Pearson, 1995; West and Zimmerman, 1983). However Kennedy and Camden's (1983) and Dindia's (1987) studies of college students did not find males more frequently interrupting females. In Dindia's study of interruptions in conversations with same- and mixed-sex dyads, both sexes interrupted opposite-sex partners more than same-sex partners, but male students did not interrupt significantly more than female students. However, in studies of families, Greif (1980) and Gleason and Greif (1983) found that fathers were more likely to interrupt children than were mothers, and both parents were more likely to interrupt girls than boys. Some researchers found women were more frequently interrupted than were men, regardless of whether women or men were doing the interrupting (Kennedy, 1980; Spender, 1980; Willis and Williams, 1976).

Many theorists and researchers have equated interruptions with attempts at conversational dominance. However, not all incidents of simultaneous speech are attempts to interrupt and control a conversation. As Kennedy (1980) and Beattie (1981) among others note, speakers may be overlapping when they express agreement and support for the previous speaker's remark or when they jump into a conversation a few syllables ahead of their conversational turn. Dindia (1987) attributes interruptions to conversational errors or awkwardness that may occur with greater frequency in mixed-sex conversations, rather than expressions of relative power. Beck (1988) and Tannen (1990) suggest that men have greater discomfort with silence, and offer this as an explanation of men's practice of interrupting others, although for an interruption to take place, one's conversational partner must be already engaged in speaking, not silently waiting her or his turn.

West and Zimmerman (1983) attempt to distinguish between those overlaps in conversation which *facilitate* a conversation and those which *disrupt* the previous speaker's turn. This distinction is significant. Few speakers feel anything other than encouragement at a conversational partner's interjection of "Yeah" or "Really?" while they are speaking. These interjections encourage a speaker to continue, rather than to give up the floor.

When analyzing the interrupting behavior of any conversational partner, it is important to consider the relationship between listening and interrupting. As the above studies indicate, the context and status of conversational interactants is a salient feature in interruptions. Persons with less power are more frequently interrupted, but power may be operationalized in a variety of different ways. In Candace West's (1984) study of communication between female doctors and male patients, for example, male dominance was a more significant factor than women's occupational status. West found that women, even those in authoritative professions, were more frequently interrupted than were men.

Vocalizers and Minimal Responses

Vocalizers and minimal responses such as "mm-hmmm," "uh-huh," "I see," and "yeah" are important parts of conversational interaction since they are frequently employed to signal attention and interest. Nichols (1948) asserted that demonstrating interest is a sign of effective listening. How we demonstrate interest, however, is also a matter of socialization.

Anthropologists Dale Maltz and Ruth Borker (1982) observed that men and women frequently use vocalizers differently. Women have been found to use vocalizers—along with nonverbal indicators of interest such as head-nodding—far more frequently than do men (Hirschman, 1973). Women are more likely to use these strategies to indicate that they are listening and to encourage the speaker to continue. Some researchers assert that men equate these behaviors with signals of agreement; therefore, they use them more sparingly. They reserve the use of vocalizers for those instances when they agree with a speaker. Although positive minimal responses provide verbal and vocal reinforcement to speakers, the absence of these signals or a delay in providing this feedback can discourage interaction. Fishman (1982) and Arliss (1991) claim that this use of minimal responses may display disinterest, because the responses may be timed after a partner's lengthy remarks and delivered in a delayed manner. Fishman finds the disconfirming use of minimal responses more common in the speech of men than women.

Whatever the actual listening and attending behavior of men and women, heterosexual women's dissatisfaction with the listening of their male partners is a well-documented fact. One of the questions in Shere Hite's (1987) study of over four thousand North American women and their love relationships was "What does your partner do that makes you the maddest?" Seventy-seven percent responded, "He doesn't listen." Further, 59 percent reported that men interrupt them; 84 percent said that men often seemed not to hear; 69 percent said that men generally did not listen or ask about activities; and 83 percent remarked that men only seemed to listen at the beginning of relationships. Interestingly, 85 percent of Hite's respondents said that the most wonderful quality of their friendships with other women was the ability to talk openly and freely without being judged. Eighty-two percent of the women in lesbian relationships said that they could talk easily and openly with their women lovers. (For a fuller discussion of gender and listening behavior, see Borisoff and Merrill, 1991, and Borisoff and Hahn, 1997b.)

However, it is important to keep in mind that neither sex nor sexuality *determines* our interaction strategies any more than it determines the verbal or vocal behaviors in which we engage. Remember that gender implies a socially learned notion of masculinity or femininity. Women may identify with some traits that are considered masculine; men may identify with some traits considered feminine. In a fascinating study on the effects of gender on conversation, Kriss Dass (1986) explored the use of "dominating" interaction patterns in communication between same sex partners. In Dass's study, ninety-one students participated in roleplays with same-sex partners. The conversations were recorded and analyzed for instances of overlap and interruption. Dass found that *regardless of the subject's sex*, the more "masculine" her or his internalized gender identity (according to the Burke and Tull gender identity measure), the greater the likelihood that a person will initiate an interruption during a conversation.

Accounting for the Communicative Behaviors: Difference or Dominance?

Clearly our patterns of speaking, listening, and responding to one another are open to various interpretations, are motivated by diverse intentions, and may be read in ways which facilitate or disrupt effective communication. Some theorists contend that different verbal behaviors observed in men and women are attributable to the fact that women have been taught to regard communication as a social medium, a mechanism for creating bonds, whereas men have been encouraged to communicate primarily to exchange information. Theorists who posit the "difference" explanation claim that tag questions, qualifiers, disclaimers, and intonation patterns that sound as though the speaker is requesting rather than commanding are strategies common to women's speech. They attribute these verbal and vocal distinctions to differences in men's and women's socialization and see the "feminine" strategies as less direct but more polite, cooperative, and inclusive than the corresponding patterns men tend to employ (Maltz and Borker, 1982; Tannen, 1987). However, these strategies are not two equal options. It must be remembered that the *need* to be polite can itself signal a power imbalance.

Brown and Levinson's (1978) discussion of politeness strategies presents a useful typology. Brown and Levinson assert that members of dominated and muted groups (including women) tend to engage in politeness strategies that affirm commonality when speaking with each other. However, politeness strategies based on avoidance and deference are more commonly used when communicating with dominant groups. Theorists who operate from a "dominance" framework when examining gender behavior remind us that subordinates who fear alienating their superiors are required to be polite. Politeness is often a strategy for gaining or maintaining favor. Those already powerful are not compelled to be polite. They can, therefore, afford to be direct. The communication behaviors regarded as masculine and feminine need to be understood within a context of male dominance, which is the primary feature of patriarchy.

In this text, we do not propose one absolute model of politeness or of directness for speakers of either sex, nor do we wish to reinforce gender-stereotyped differences in speech. We see neither model as inherently weak nor strong. Rather, we hope that all individuals might increase their repertoire of strategies and responses, and understand each in their larger social contexts. As a way of encouraging more collaborative and less hierarchical exchanges, we suggest the following three strategies:

1. First, in every interruption or overlap, there is an interrupter and a person who concedes to the interruption. The person being interrupted need not acquiesce. She or he may continue speaking or calmly state, "You interrupted me. I haven't finished speaking yet." Communicators who are repeatedly informed that they interrupt others need to take responsibility for the fact that they are conveying a metacommunicative message that their own words are of more importance than those of their conversational partner.

2. Second, when attempting to initiate or develop a topic and receiving only few or delayed minimal responses, the first member of a dyad might revise his or her questioning strategies by asking increasingly more open questions. For example, if the response to "Was your presentation successful?" is "Uh-huh," the initiator who wants to engage in a full conversation might ask direct questions, such as "What aspects of your presenta-

tion were most well- received?" Listeners who provide their conversational partners with little feedback should consider their part in the process of negotiating and engaging in topic selection, rather than maintaining "veto" power through withholding responses.

3. Finally, all listeners need to be aware of the verbal and vocal encouragement they provide while someone is speaking. When speakers feel that their listeners are distracted or that attention is being withheld, they should stop their communicative attempt and identify the *disconfirming responses* they are receiving before the interaction continues.

Evelyn Sieburg and Carl Larson (1971) examined seven types of responses in which one speaker ignored some significant aspect of another speaker's message. Their research did not specifically investigate gender differences, but informal observations in our classrooms have led us to note that the following disconfirming behaviors frequently are present in mixed-sex dyads.

1. **The impervious response**. In the impervious response, the speaker's comment is ignored verbally and nonverbally. Women often complain that in a meeting, a suggestion that was ignored when they voiced it was later adopted enthusiastically when offered by a male colleague. Women, children, minorities, the aged, the physically challenged—all the less powerful segments of our society—find their messages met, all too frequently, with impervious responses. The resultant feeling of being "invisible" is extremely frustrating.

2. **The interrupting response**. As we have discussed above, the interrupting response is also a negation of a speaker's communicative attempt. Sieburg and Larson (1971) identify interruptions that are not prefaced by such injections as "I understand, however . . ." as particularly disconfirming.

3. **The irrelevant response**. The irrelevant response occurs when a listener makes a comment totally unrelated to what the other person was just saying. This is one of the ways more powerful members of a dyad or a group attempt to control the selection of topics and to dominate discussions.

4. **The tangential response**. Related to the irrelevant response is the tangential one. In this case, a speaker nominally acknowledges the other speaker's message, but then shifts the conver-

sation in another direction of his or her own choosing. An example of this type of response follows:

EMPLOYEE: I'd like to talk with you about my upcoming promotion.

EMPLOYER: Sure, I know you want a raise, but now you'd better concentrate on your current project so that we don't get backlogged.

5. ***The impersonal response***. This refers to a generalized, intellectualized response to a speaker's message. An impersonal response may be a categorical assertion, such as the response of the manager in the following exchange:

UNION REPRESENTATIVE: I think we should have daycare facilities available on the premises for children of employees.

MANAGER: Women want it both ways. You can't be a good worker and a good mother. Something has to give.

6. ***The ambiguous response***. In this kind of interaction, the respondent is intentionally vague and may be misleading the first speaker. For example:

WORKER: Am I next in line for a supervisory position?

MANAGER: Could be. I'm not really sure how these things work.

7. ***The incongruous response***. In this exchange the verbal and nonverbal components of the respondent's message appear to contradict each other:

CLIENT: Are you upset that I'm late for my appointment?

PRACTITIONER: (*shouting and banging on the desk*) No, I'm **not** upset.

All of these disconfirming responses disparage and discourage the communicative attempts of speakers while fostering and reinforcing a power differential. Dominating speakers have the power to "disconfirm" the messages of subordinates. All of us need to be able to identify and to eliminate these behaviors if we are to have more harmonious personal and professional interactions.

Further, we do not want to reify as "normal" or "desirable" those communicative behaviors associated with men and masculinity, nor do we expect women and members of marginalized groups of both sexes to bear the responsibility of understanding, decoding, and adapting to the models of more dominant others. Early gender difference researchers operated from this "deficit theory." We recognize that most of the disparities reported in empirical studies of men's and women's communication—whether anecdotal or actual—serve to reinforce and perhaps even to perpetuate power imbalances associated with gender stereotypes. Whatever the actual incidence of gender differences in any specific study or communicative exchange, we contend, along with Deaux and Major (1987), that the "enactment of gender primarily takes place within the context of social interaction, either explicitly or implicitly" (p. 370), and so our vocal and verbal behaviors as communicators may be considered the "stage" on which we perform the micropolitical communicative acts which constitute gender.

Suggested Activities

A. Focus on Listening

Rousseau's quotation, which prefaces this chapter, motivated Mary Wollstonecraft in 1791 to write her historic *Vindication of the Rights of Woman* in rebuttal.

Whereas Rousseau enjoined women by "art" or artifice to render themselves agreeable to men, Wollstonecraft wished

> . . . to persuade women to endeavor to acquire strength, both of mind and body, and to convince them that the *soft phrases*, susceptibility of heart, delicacy of sentiment and refinement of taste, *are almost synonymous with epithets of weakness*, and *that those beings who are only the objects of pity* and that kind of love, which has been termed its sister, *will soon become objects of contempt.*[emphasis added]

Mary Wollstonecraft
Introduction to First Edition
A Vindication of the Rights of Woman

Observe individuals who employ the submissive gestures (discussed in chapter 1) and the self-trivializing speech patterns identified in this chapter as mechanisms for making themselves agreeable or to gain the approval of their superiors. Using the chart on the following page, enter the strategies used and whether their superiors respond in the desired fashion or dismiss the communication with "pity" or, as Wollstonecraft claims, with "contempt."

Speaker	Message Intended	Strategy Employed	Listener	Listener's Reaction

B. Focus on Dyadic Communication

In pairs, role play an imaginary dialogue between Rousseau and Wollstonecraft or contemporary equivalents like Phyllis Schlafly and Gloria Steinem. Switch roles and attempt to defend the opposite position.

C. Focus on Small Group Communication: Interpersonal

In a small group, with equal numbers of male and female members, discuss a controversial social topic in front of an audience. For the purpose of the exercise, all the male members should employ the traditional feminine strategies (e.g., tag questions, qualifiers, disclaimers, etc.) and the female members should use categorical assertions and other masculine styles. After the discussion, ask the class or seminar group to evaluate each member according to the following criteria:

Agree   **Disagree**
1   2   3   4   5
Vocal, Verbal, and Nonverbal Behavior

1. Member was an effective speaker.
2. Member was an effective listener.
3. Member seemed well prepared.
4. Member seemed authoritative.
5. Member seemed sensitive to communicative behavior of other group members.

D. Focus on Communication: Exercises to Lower Pitch

To open up and speak from the lower range of your natural pitch, practice by sitting in a chair and placing a book on the floor in front of you. Lean over limply, with your head between your legs, and read aloud into the floor. Tape yourself in this position. You will hear yourself speaking from the bottom reaches of your voice. Try to maintain this while in an upright position.

In order to maintain the lower pitch, place your hand low on your chest while you speak. By focusing your concentration lower in your chest instead of in a constricted throat, you will remind yourself to bring your pitch down.

Chapter Three

Gender and Nonverbal Communication

The effect of gender is produced through the stylization of the body and, hence, must be understood as the mundane way in which bodily gestures, movements, and styles of various kinds constitute the illusion of an abiding gendered self.

— Judith Butler, *Gender Trouble*

There's language in her eye, her cheek, her lip; Nay, her foot speaks; Her wanton spirits look out at every joint and motive of her body.

— Shakespeare, *Troilus and Cressida*

According to Judith Butler (1990), what we know as gender is a set of "acts" or social performances which people are repeatedly compelled to enact so that, over time, they "produce the appearance of substance, of a natural sort of being" (p. 33). For example, young girls are intentionally taught to "sit like a lady" with legs close together; young boys are instructed not to cry or express fear. Erving Goffman (1979) has called these nonverbal behaviors a form of "gender display." There are frequently severe social penalties for those who act in violation of their culture's accepted gender "script." The gender-differentiated nonverbal behaviors that result from this socialization are learned rather than. innate, and they become part of an individual's experience as a "gendered self." As a result, many people conclude that men "naturally" take up more space than do women or that women are "naturally" more emotionally expressive than men, although the prescriptions for how men and women should act vary from culture to culture.

Nonverbal messages have a *presentational* dimension; it is through demeanor, gestures, expressions, and artifacts that communicators present aspects of their socially constructed—and gendered—selves to others. It is through our nonverbal behaviors that we express and display our emotions and our experience of gender, ethnicity, sexuality, and socioeconomic class identifications. Each of these variables influences the others. For example, every culture formulates its own display rules that dictate when, how, and with what consequences nonverbal expressions will be exhibited. In some cultures, heterosexual male friends, family members, or colleagues routinely walk hand-in-hand and kiss each other upon greeting and leave-taking; but in other cultures men who engage in these behaviors are considered homosexual. In some cultures, women are taught that it is not "ladylike" to run, to meet a man's gaze directly, or to expose one's arms, legs, or face to the gaze of male strangers in public. In other cultures, women engage in athletics and wear slacks and shirts with short sleeves, clothing that is not differentiated from that worn by men.

In this chapter, we will examine some of the assumptions and controversies about the nonverbal performance of gender as well as explore women's and men's use and interpretation of such nonverbal variables as space, height, touch, gesture, facial expressions, and eye contact. Further, because sensitivity to the nonverbal messages of others is both a learned skill and related to a given society's gender expectations, we will consider whether men and women differ in their perception of and ability to decode nonverbal messages accurately.

SPACE, OR "BIGGER IS BETTER"

In North American culture, space is a signifier of power, and individuals who have command over greater amounts of space and territory are often considered to have greater power. Women and lower-status persons of both sexes are afforded and expected to take up less space than males and higher-status persons. In addition, people in subordinate positions cannot control others from entering the space available to them. The boss can enter the worker's space, lean on the employee's desk, or tower over the subordinate. Only with the supervisor's invitation can the subordinate enter into the supervisor's space. In public and in private, in the workplace and in the streets, women constantly experience space encroachment. Gender-differentiated proxemic patterns appear even in childhood when young boys are encouraged and permitted to play outdoors while play for young girls is more frequently centered within the home (Graebner, 1982; Harper and Sanders, 1985; Thorne, 1993; Valentine, 1997).

Learned behavior patterns inform beliefs about entitlement to space and affect how individuals interpret the use of space—especially when expected spatial norms are violated. In the animal kingdom and among human beings, subordinates yield space to dominants. Frank Willis (1966) performed studies in which he measured the initial distance set by an approaching person. He established that both sexes approach women more closely than they do men. In a review of many such research studies on nonverbal sex differences in interpersonal distance, Judith Hall (1984) also found that females are approached more closely than are males. When women's space is intruded upon, they are apt to acquiesce to the intrusion—just as they frequently acquiesce to interruptions. Jeanette Silveira's research (1972) indicated that when men and women walked toward each other on the sidewalk, the woman moved out of the man's way in twelve out of nineteen cases. Knapp and Hall (1997) speculate that acquiescing or ceding space to males may be linked, in part, to associating male behavior with the potential for threatening aggression. They further hypothesize that acquiescence to "invasions" of personal space may be attributed to societal norms for maintaining "appropriate" distance; "people expect men to keep larger distances, and when they do not, it may be disturbing" (p. 168). Yet as we have seen, societal norms and expectations serve dominant interests.

Women are encouraged to sit and move in ways that intensify the lesser amount of space available to them. For example, women when involved in a dyadic or small-group communication interaction may sit poised on the edge of a chair, eagerly leaning forward rather than "taking up" space. "Feminine" clothes also contribute to a nonverbal image of female weakness and reconfigure the bodies that wear them. Tight skirts and tight slacks restrict movement. High heels force women to take small steps. In the late 1800s economist Thorstein Veblen (1899) asserted that "the high heel, the skirt, the impracticable bonnet, the corset, and the general disregard of the wearer's comfort which is an obvious feature of all civilized women's apparel, are so many items of evidence to the effect that in the modern civilized scheme of life the woman is still, in theory, the economic dependent of the man." Veblen noted that middle-class women were not just restricted in their movements, they, and their relative powerlessness, were literally "on display" (p. 126–27).

In the United States, contemporary women are still socialized to take up less space than men. They are taught to sit with their legs together and elbows to their sides and to walk with smaller steps. Contemporary women's fashion, such as tight clothing, short skirts, and high heels, discourages women who wear it from sitting and moving expansively, as do men. While seated, men spread their legs and put their arms on the armrests of chairs. They walk with longer strides. We know that these stereotypical ways of moving are not anatomically based, because men in Asia, for example, sit with their legs as closely together and cross their legs as do Western women. Yet in the United States, men who retreat into such little available space may not be considered "masculine," while women who sit and stand with open movements and walk with long strides may be regarded as "unfeminine."

Culture as well as gender exerts a determining force on the degree of personal space individuals use in interaction with each other. Members of many cultures tend, in general, to interact at closer distances than do white North Americans. As Carol Zinner Dolphin (1988) has established, "use of personal space as influenced by the sex(es) of interacting individuals tends to differ dramatically from one culture to another" (p. 28). Dolphin found that proximity was influenced by a given culture's expectations for male or female behavior. Thus, while one culture may expect physical closeness and contact between men, in another this may be largely forbidden. Some cultures may expect women to maintain larger distances from each other than are expected of men from each other, while members of other cultures may interpret such behavior between women as a sign of coldness or disinterest. While some cultures allow for a degree of close physical proximity in mixed-sex interactions, others prohibit it and proscribe greater amounts of distance between men and women.

Jeffrey Sanders and his colleagues (1985) studied the degrees of personal distance maintained between same- and mixed-sex dyads of North American and Arab students. Sanders found that mixed-sex pairs of Arab women and men interacted at a much greater distance than did either same-sex pairs of Arab students or same- or mixed-sex North American pairs. Robert Shuter's (1976) study of proxemics and touch in men and women from three Latin American cultures (Costa Rica, Colombia, and Panama) found that same-sex female dyads in all three cultures interacted the most closely—at significantly smaller distances and with greater amounts of physical contact—than same-sex male or opposite-sex dyads. In these two cases, respectively, the greater distance between men and women and the greater closeness between women are cultural expectations, constituting part of the construction and performance of gender in the cultures studied.

Within most cultures, the closer people feel to each other emotionally, the more they are likely to allow each other to be close in proximity. Thus, the distance between communicators in an interaction may be influenced by gender, culture, power, and the degree of intimacy and reciprocity. There is no one meaning for any given nonverbal message. In some cases, close interpersonal distances between people are a result of warmth and affiliation; in others, they reflect an abuse of status differences. Distance between partners in an interaction may be an expression of respect and deference—or disinterest and hostility.

Lombardo's (1986) study of sex-roles and personal distance has led him to suggest that the sex of communicators and their orientation toward particular sex roles exerts a considerable impact over how individuals use space, their perceptions of spatial needs, and the invasions of their personal space. For example, as we will see in chapter 5, if the feeling of emotional closeness or affiliation between individuals is not reciprocal, an undesired intrusion into others' personal space may be considered a gross abuse of power. Our discussion of sexual harassment will be informed by an awareness of the complex components involved in such nonverbal behavior as negotiating personal space. According to Bochner (1982), the "meanings" attached to the use of personal space are determined by a range of variables, including the relationship between the individuals involved, their relative status and power, their degree of intimacy, and the type of activity in which they are engaged.

TOUCH, OR "JUST A FRIENDLY PAT ON THE BACK?"

Touch, like physical closeness, may be considered an expression of affection, support, or sexual attraction. However, touch may be used to express and maintain an asymmetrical relationship as well as a reciprocal one. For example, as a gesture of comfort, the doctor may touch the patient, but the patient may not initiate physical contact with the doctor. Similarly, upon entering the secretary's cubicle, the department head might pat the secretary on the back and inquire about her or his family. However, this apparently "friendly" gesture is not as benign as it appears as long as the secretary does not have an equal right to initiate the same pat on the back and elicit similar personal information from the department head. As we shall see in chapter 5, undesired touch in the workplace can be a form of harassment.

In the mid-1970s, Nancy Henley performed observational studies investigating the relationship between touch and socioeconomic status, sex, and age. Henley (1973, 1977) found that, in interactions between people not romantically involved with each other, higher-status persons (individuals of higher socioeconomic status, male, and older) touched lower-status persons significantly more often. In their review of gender and touching behavior between romantic partners, Knapp and Hall (1997) report "inconsistent" findings on "which sex touches the other more, overall" (p. 303). In these situations, as a relationship becomes more intimate and committed, sex differences in the initiation of touch between partners appears less evident. Yet even in such relationships, Knapp and Hall contend that "observers seem to *perceive* the initiator [of touch] as the person with greater power" (p. 304).These findings have important implications for both women and men. Individuals of both sexes should guard against using touch to assert authority. We should avoid initiating touch in situations where either the other individual is not desirous of the gesture or where the higher-status person would not accept a reciprocal touch.

What about when the gesture *is* reciprocal? Coworkers must be aware of outsiders possibly misconstruing the sexual implications of touch. In the 1984 Mondale-Ferraro campaign for the United States presidency, newscasters mentioned a distinction from previous campaigns. Whereas male candidates for president and vice-president traditionally linked inner arms and waved their raised outer arms, Mondale and Ferraro waved outer arms with their inner arms at their sides. They did not touch each other. The sexism and heterosexism in our society impose restrictions on behavior. Until people become accustomed to perceiving women as competent professionals in their own right rather than as potential sexual objects, they will have difficulty imagining a collegial relationship between men and women without sexual implications. Consequently, at present, women and men who work together will continue to be subject to greater scrutiny than same-sex pairs.

Within same-sex dyads in the United States, women are generally much freer than men to touch one another. Women friends and relatives may walk arm-in-arm, dance together, and hug one another. Touch between heterosexual males is generally more restricted. As Barrie Thorne (1993) found in her ethnographic study of elementary school boys and girls, young girls regularly engage in such gestures of intimacy with each other as stroking or combing their friends' hair, whereas touch among boys is rarely relaxed and affectionate—limited primarily to a ritual handslap and the mock violence of pushing, poking, and grabbing (p. 94). Outside of the sporting arena, many North American men do not feel free to exchange much more than a slap on the back without their behavior being construed as having sexual connotations.

It is important to remember that the notion of "appropriate" touch, like that of "comfortable" interpersonal distance between communicators, is largely culturally determined. In some cultures same-sex male dyads have a greater latitude of haptic expression with each other. They may commonly hug or kiss each other on both cheeks, for example, while women friends or family members are much more restricted in their socially sanctioned ability to touch one another. In some cultures, all touch between men and women who are not related to each other by family or by marriage is strictly forbidden. In these circumstances, uninvited touch may be experienced as an abuse of power that takes the form of cultural as well as sexual oppression.

HEIGHT, OR "WHOM DO YOU LOOK UP TO?"

Height is also a nonverbal variable that may be manipulated, thereby either empowering or impeding an individual. We say, "I look up to you" to indicate respect or admiration. "Higher," like "bigger," is often used to mean "better" or "more" (as in "higher class," "high opinion").

In hierarchies, the individual with greater power frequently is perceived as taller than he or she is. Paul R. Wilson (1968) reported that undergraduates who were asked to estimate the height of a man who was described as any one of five academic ranks increased their estimation of his height when his ascribed status was increased. In some environments—for example, in courtrooms, in the military, in some religious practices—deference is enforced by norms of courtesy and respect which dictate, for example, who may sit and who may stand when status unequals interact.

While men as a group may be somewhat taller than women, in individual mixed-sex dyads, these differences may be minimal or reversed. However, there are behaviors which make males appear taller. Social dyads in which the woman is appreciably taller than the man are frequently subject to ridicule, as though they are subverting gender and power expectations. In a world in which height equals power and women are not supposed to be more powerful than men, taller women may attempt to diminish themselves, to slouch and round their shoulders so as to retreat or to occupy as little space as possible.

Traditional female facial expressions of coyness and flirtation may reinforce the height and power differential between the sexes. For example, women frequently exhibit their femininity by tilting their heads to the side and looking upward when talking to male conversational partners. Although the head tilt is a gesture which indicates attentive listening in either sex, women are apt to employ this more frequently in mixed-sex pairs than men, thus reinforcing the notion that, in addition to listening, the woman is "looking up to" the man.

We must guard against using height to control or to influence. Superiors need not tower over subordinates in the workplace. Tall individuals should be encouraged neither to use their height in an intimidating fashion nor to attempt to diminish themselves by denying their personal power. Power need not be used as power *over* others.

FACIAL EXPRESSIONS, OR "YOU LOOK SO PRETTY WHEN YOU SMILE"

White, middle-class women in the United States are expected to be highly expressive emotionally. One of the hallmarks of the feminine stereotype for this group is to be facially expressive, and a woman's face is believed to reflect her emotional state. The most common and easily discernible facial expression is the smile.

From childhood, white female children are admonished to smile. They are taught to smile not as an expression of their own pleasure, but because it is pleasing to others. Hence a smile may be considered a gesture of appeasement or deference. Women are told that they are more attractive when they smile and appear happy. The key word in the previous sentence is "appear." As long as women and other subordinates are concerned with pleasing others, they are not considered threatening to their superiors. African-American women are not expected to perform their "femininity" within their cultures in exactly the same manner. As a result, Halberstadt and Saitta (1987) found African-American women to be less deferential than white women and, therefore, less inclined to smile merely because it is expected of them. Consequently, some of the racism to which women of color are exposed is a result of whites misinterpreting an absence of facial gestures of deference as hostility, arrogance, unfriendliness, or disinterest. As long as one *seems* to be satisfied with the position that has been allotted, the hierarchical system is reinforced. Smiles, therefore, can function as genuine or artificial signs of satisfaction.

In addition to functioning as an expression of pleasure, pleasantness, or a desire for approval, smiling may also reflect the smiler's nervousness. In a number of service occupations, smiling is not only preferred behavior, it is *required*. In Arlie Russell Hochschild's (1983) article "Smile Wars: Counting the Casualties of Emotional Labor," she discussed the emotional labor required of flight attendants. According to Hochschild, the flight attendant, receptionist, waitress, and salesperson often pay a psychological price for their requisite smiles. When a smile is an *expected* part of the job, it becomes a commodity to be given. Women in these and other occupations frequently are required to "give" male patrons or superiors a smile. The constant feigned smile is an expression of duplicity. (And it must be feigned, for obviously no one can be happy all the time.) An individual engaging in this behavior cuts him- or herself off from the expression of his or her own emotions. The smile becomes a mask, a form of "make up," constructed to gain the approval of one who has power. Subordinates are expected to smile at superiors. When the boss walks into the room, the secretaries are expected to smile and warmly greet him or her.

Moreover, dominant members of a hierarchy are less likely to smile or disclose their feelings nonverbally. (See chapter 2 for our discussion of verbal self-disclosure.) They typically withhold verbal and nonverbal expressions of emotions. Instead, they are often encouraged to maintain a "poker face," to appear neutral and impassive, and to disclose as little about themselves as possible. However, in some contexts, rather than smiling to gain others' approval, superiors are apt to assume facial expressions which imply that they are judging others. One such example, according to Gerald I. Nierenberg and Henry H. Calero (1971), is the disapproving attitude conveyed by raised eyebrows, a partially twisted head, and a look of doubt. (According to Webster's Dictionary, the word *supercilious* comes from Latin meaning "disdain or haughtiness as expressed by raising the eyebrows.")

Little difference has been found in the smiling behavior of female and male infants and young children. However, as white North American girls grow up, they smile significantly more frequently than do white North American boys. In one study, preschool boys' spontaneous facial expressions were found to decrease dramatically from age four to six (Buck, 1977). According to Hall (1984), "this suggests that socialization, pressure or modeling induces boys during this period to reduce expression of emotion via the face" (p. 54). The social pressure to present a "more masculine" face (less smiling) may be operative for boys at this age since they are likely to be in school starting at age four or five.

As we stated earlier, women are believed to be more facially expressive (Hall 1984; Leathers 1986) than men. In analyses of numerous studies of expression accuracy, Hall (1984) found that "females were better expressors, that is their expressions were more accurately judged by decoders" (p. 53). Perhaps one of the ways to account for women's greater expressiveness is to consider to what extent the performance of femininity in the United States depends upon heightened or exaggerated facial expression.

Zuckerman and his colleagues (1982) conducted three separate studies which related the legibility of an individual's facial expressions to signifiers of masculinity and femininity. The studies revealed that the very concept of femininity implies clear and willing expression of nonverbal cues. According to Marianne La France and Nancy Henley (1994) the pressure on women to develop and to "perform" these nonverbal cues is reinforced and perpetuated by men's "greater social power relative to women in everyday social interactions" (p. 290). Borisoff and Hahn (1997a) contend that to the extent that initial attractiveness and heterosexual relationship satisfaction remain associated with women's nonverbal expressiveness, women "are destined to be the arbiters of affective nonverbal display" (p. 65). Of course, nonverbal signifiers of "masculinity" or "femininity" are culturally determined, rather than innate. In those cultures and subcultures in which being facially expressive is an integral component in the collection of behaviors that are seen as markers of "femininity," males may resist both the nonverbal display of expression and attentiveness to others in order to appear more masculine.

As Buck (1979) has noted, people whose faces express their emotional states have lower levels of electrothermal response than do people whose faces do not display emotion. Higher electrothermal responses indicate suppressed emotions and have been considered possible contributors to heart disease and other stress-related conditions which are more prevalent in men than women. Thus, men may be paying with their lives for withholding emotional expression (see Borisoff and Merrill, 1991).

As we will see in the following chapters, in homes, schools, and workplaces we need to be aware of ways in which expressions of emotions serve to establish or maintain a power differential. Women and other subordinates should evaluate the need to engage in overeager smiles for approval or to offer smiles that are expected of them. Men and dominant members of hierarchies should also reevaluate their tendency to withhold or mask emotional expressiveness and equate the appearance of pleasing expressions with compliance due them. They might also allow themselves to engage more openly in genuine, mutual expressions of pleasure and approval.

GAZE, OR "ARE YOU LOOKING AT ME?"

Direct eye contact between individuals may be interpreted in several different ways. Looking directly into another person's eyes can connote an aggressive threat, a sexual invitation, or a desire for honest and open communication. For many contemporary theorists, the "gaze" is a metaphor for power, where a seeing subject—frequently assumed to be male—takes the position of an active spectator when regarding another person as a passive object. This notion of objectification, where one person looks while another "is looked at," is at the root of many interpretations of and reactions to eye contact.

A number of years ago, actor Robert DeNiro portrayed a psychopathic murderer in the film *Taxi Driver*. Posed in front of a mirror, DeNiro glared at his own reflection, taunting an imaginary assailant whom he envisioned to be staring at him. Menacingly, he asked, ". . . You talkin' to me? Who do you think you're talkin' to?" DeNiro's character interpreted a glance as an attempt at dominance. Researchers Ellsworth, Carlsmith, and Henson (1972) tell us that a stare may have this function. Ellsworth and her colleagues have reported studies that relate staring in humans to primate threat displays. For most individuals, a glance that catches another person's eye for several seconds is relatively insignificant. If, however, eye contact is maintained beyond several seconds, a nonverbal power contest may ensue in which the person with less power ultimately averts her or his eyes.

Thus, gaze has been proven to be related to status and power as well as to gender. In a number of cultures, children are taught that to look adults in the eyes is a sign of disrespect. Submission is indicated by a bowed head and an averted glance. In mixed-sex pairs, women are more likely than men to avert their eyes. Judith Hall's (1984) analysis established that "the more dominant individual gazes more while speaking and relatively less while listening; while the less dominant individual gazes more while listening and relatively less while speaking" (p. 73). Further, Ellyson and his colleagues' 1980 study on visual dominance behavior in female dyads found that while women with relatively high status gazed an equivalent amount of time while speaking and listening, lower-status female subjects gazed significantly more while listening than when speaking. In her book *Body Politics*, Nancy Henley attempted to differentiate between subordinate attentiveness and dominant staring. Henley (1977) claimed that women and other subordinates look at others more but avert their eyes when looked at. Both of these behaviors are indicative of submissiveness. Status exerts a powerful influence on gaze and affects the behavior of research subjects of both sexes. Knapp and Hall (1997) reported that in studies where the variable of assigned status was removed "the male tends to use the gaze pattern typically used by higher-status people, while the female tends to use the gaze pattern typically used by lower-status people" (p. 456).

In any discussion of nonverbal communication, it is important not to interpret behavior in an ethnocentric fashion. Eye contact, like all other nonverbal behavior, has different connotations in different cultural contexts. There are cultures in which direct eye contact between men and women is regarded as a sexual invitation and is, therefore, to be avoided in "polite" society. For individuals from these backgrounds, averting one's eyes in a mixed-sex dyad may be a sign of respect, modesty, or disinterest, rather than inattentiveness or submissiveness. In Curt and Nine's (1983) study of nonverbal communication among Hispanic couples, they found that many Puerto Rican wives never looked directly at their husbands.

Because of differing expectations and interpretations for behavior, there is the potential for much misunderstanding in mixed-sex and intercultural communication exchanges. Women and men need to be able to identify very precisely those behaviors which seem intrusive or inappropriate and their connection with power inequities in specific social contexts.

GESTURE AND DEMEANOR, OR "ACT LIKE A LADY"

It is through our bearing, demeanor, and gestural mannerisms that we perform much of the behavior that is associated with gender identities. But the gestures of communicators, the ways they "carry themselves," and the meanings associated with those nonverbal behaviors are also, in part, culturally specific, and they have changed over time.

In a nineteenth-century English etiquette manual entitled *The Habits of Good Society : A Handbook for Ladies and Gentlemen* (1870), readers who desired "good manners" were warned that "Foreigners talk with their arms and hands as auxiliaries to the voice. The custom is considered vulgar by us calm Englishmen. . . . You have no need to act with the hands, but if you use them at all, it should be very slightly and gracefully, never bringing down your fist upon the table, nor slapping one hand upon the other, nor poking your fingers at your interlocutor" (pp. 284–85). Yet, while appearing "calm" and "graceful" might signify appropriate "manly" gentility to the Englishman of one hundred years ago, those same qualities of graceful restraint are liable to be read as "feminine" to contemporary North American communicators who have been taught to equate forcefulness with "masculinity" rather than vulgarity. Class and cultural biases are apparent in this warning not to "talk with one's hands." Similar gender biases and stereotypes are operative when women are told that it is "ladylike" to stand up straight and hold one's body rigid, rather than to appear to be "loose" and "easy," as if a woman's deportment signified her sexual availability.

ARTIFACTUAL MESSAGES, OR "WHAT YOU WEAR SPEAKS VOLUMES"

Artifacts are objects. When worn, they have been used to signify a wearer's gender, culture, and socioeconomic class. From the moment at which families or hospitals assign infants pink or blue blankets, artifacts announce and contribute to the shaping of children's experience of gender. As Julia Wood (1994) has noted, clothing is a form of artifactual communication that "manifest[s] and promote[s] cultural definitions of masculinity and femininity" (p. 159). In earlier centuries sumptuary laws regulated "appropriate" dress, and it was literally against the law for women to wear men's breeches, for men to appear in women's dress, or for anyone to dress above their appropriate "station" in life by wearing the clothes of others more privileged than they, except in the special province of the theatre (Garber, 1992; Merrill, 1998 in press).

Elizabeth Grosz (1994) has asserted that "through exercise and habitual patterns of movement, through negotiating its environment . . . and through clothing and make-up, the body is more or less marked, constituted as an appropriate, or, as the case may be, inappropriate body for its cultural requirements." Grosz contends that these procedures are more than adornment; rather, the "norms and ideals governing beauty and health" in a given culture and time literally shape the bodies of those who ascribe to them (p. 142). Consider the nineteenth-century woman tightly lacing herself into a corset designed to reduce her waist to a then-fashionable eighteen inches, and so transforming her body into an artificial hourglass shape, or the contemporary man using steroids to build his muscles into a body type currently fashionable. In both cases norms of "beauty" and people's complicity in or resistance to them send complex messages about gender and cultural values. What do the bodies of bodybuilders or anorexics "communicate" about the desirability of hard, pumped-up muscles or excessively thin, childlike bodies to those who witness them?

Like other forms of nonverbal communication, our bodies and the ways we clothe them are liable to be interpreted to signify things that the communicator may not have intended. For example, women are frequently seen and evaluated largely in terms of how they appear to others. Whether or not women's bodies are clothed in such a way as to intentionally draw attention to female body parts, sex-differentiated clothing (such as low-cut blouses, tightly fitted garments, short skirts, and high heels), rather than merely reflecting an individual's taste and sense of personal aesthetics, reinforces cultural values. Men's looser fitting clothing, ample pockets, and flat shoes afford those who wear them a greater freedom of movement than most women's clothes.

DECODING NONVERBAL MESSAGES, OR "I CAN SEE WHAT YOU MEAN"

In Judith Hall's (1984) extensive review of studies of differences in decoding nonverbal messages, women were found to be significantly better decoders of nonverbal cues than were men. Women were found to be most skilled in decoding facial expressions. Hall based her review on seventy-five studies of sex differences in nonverbal decoding skills and fifty subsequent studies (1984) as well as her work with Robert Rosenthal on the design of the PONS (Profile of Nonverbal Sensitivity) Test. Regardless of age, white and African-American women exceeded men in the ability to ascertain emotions expressed nonverbally. Although differences in men's and women's scores on the PONS Test were small, they were consistent. Recent research, according to Knapp and Hall (1997) suggests no discernable differences in the ability to determine solely from nonverbal cues whether or not an individual is lying. The only emotion Knapp and Hall found men to be more adept at identifying was anger in other men.

To what can we attribute this facility? Several different hypotheses have been offered. Rosenthal and his colleagues (1979) hypothesized that women's greater accuracy in decoding facial expressions may be related to the fact that women gaze at others' faces more in interaction and that "one decodes better what one is paying attention to at the moment" (Hall 1984, p. 34). Related to this is the claim that women's experience with young children and their sensitivity as caregivers necessitate their accurate reading of nonverbal messages (Rosenthal et al., 1979).

Hall proposed a relationship between the amount of time that women gaze at their conversational partners and women's greater accuracy in decoding facial expressions. She suggested that "women may seek cues of approval or disapproval or cues that indicate how contented others are from moment to moment as part of a general motive to maintain harmonious relationships" (1984, pp. 34–35). Furthermore, research findings support a positive correlation between an individual's successful decoding of nonverbal cues and that individual's own expression accuracy in depicting messages nonverbally. Thus, women, who themselves are expected to be more nonverbally expressive, may be more accurate in reading the messages of others.

Nancy Henley (1973, 1977) offered the "oppression" theory. She posited that women, and others who have less power, must learn to "read" the nonverbal messages of those who have power over them. People who are oppressed have heightened needs to anticipate and to understand others' nonverbal messages. Henley claims that this is the reason for the greater interpersonal sensitivity of women and other less dominant persons. We suspect, therefore, that as women and men continue to negotiate and redefine their social roles and economic positions in society, these changes are likely to influence acuity in decoding nonverbal messages. At this point, however, Hall and her colleagues' findings that women far exceeded men in their ability to ascertain emotions expressed nonverbally remains largely uncontested in the research literature.

It appears impossible to provide one definitive explanation for women's greater facility with decoding nonverbal messages. Basically, all of the explanations offered to date fall into two categories: theorists who relate women's greater nonverbal decoding skills to needs which arise out of their subordinate status and theorists who attribute women's nonverbal skills to their greater tendency toward affiliation with others. However, as Hall contends:

> . . . it is . . . difficult to disentangle these two basic explanations—dominance and affiliation—because of the possibility that women's lower status reduces their ability to challenge or threaten anyone, which in turn enables or requires them to act warm and nice. (1984, p. 84)

In any case, nonverbal factors such as touch, space, height, gaze, and facial expressions exert a potent influence on our interactions with others. Although frequently unacknowledged, many of our notions of masculinity and femininity rest on the nonverbal messages we display and those we decode. We are often unaware of our nonverbal behavior and of how it is being interpreted by others. This can present obstacles in professional as well as personal settings. Certainly one cannot work effectively if being ogled or ignored, leered at or laughed at. We need to monitor our own behavior responsibly and to provide feedback to others about what we perceive to be their reactions to us.

Suggested Activities

A. Focus on Small Group Communication: Height and Power Differential

In the midst of a conversation in an informal setting with a group of friends or family members, situate yourself at a different height than your companions. If everyone is sitting in chairs, sit on the floor or stand up. Maintain your part of the conversation. Note people's nonverbal reactions to you. How long does it take until someone else in the group is "on your level"?

B. Focus on Intercultural Settings

The class will divide into groups composed of 5 to 6 members, with a mix of men and women in each group. Each group's task is to create a fictional culture with its own nonverbal norms and behaviors for each sex (allow approximately 20 minutes for this process). Once the groups have established their behaviors, one representative from each group "visits" another group and engages in conversation while using all of the nonverbal behaviors that are operative from the fictional culture of the visitor's group. The members of the "host" group try to discern the rules, norms, and roles of the visitor's culture.

C. Focus on Nonverbal Stereotyping

The professor or group leader brings in several pictures from magazine ads/articles showing women and men in different professional and personal settings. The pictures are taped to the board at the front of the room. Write a brief fictional account about each figure's life. Discuss how you and others in the group or class arrived at the fictional lives of the figures in the photos. The extent to which the figures display gender-stereotyped gestures and artifacts may also be addressed.

D. Focus on Touch

Keep a personal log of all of the touches you observe or receive during a two- to three-day period. Using the chart on the following page, identify the initiator of the touch, the situation, the status relationship between the initiator and the recipient, the sex of each, the appropriateness of the touch, and the recipient's reaction.

Initiator of the Touch	Situation	Status of Initiator v. Recipient/Sex of Each	Perceived Appropriateness of the Touch	Recipient's Reaction

Chapter Four

Gendered Scripts
Early Socialization in the Home and School

All our human scheme of things rests on the same tacit assumption: man being held the human type; woman a sort of accompaniment and subordinate assistant, merely essential to the making of people. She has held always the place of a preposition in relation to man. She has always been considered above him or below him, before him, behind him, beside him, a wholly relative existence—"Sydney's sister," "Pembroke's mother"—but never by any chance Sydney or Pembroke herself.

> — Charlotte Perkins Gilman, *The Man-Made World; or, Our Androcentric Culture*

In her text, Charlotte Perkins Gilman (1911/1971) suggests that women have been viewed in relation to or in comparison with men. The previous chapters examined how the communicative behaviors associated with men and masculinity have developed as the presumed standard or norm and how the communication styles and strategies associated with women have been regarded and valued in relation to this presumed standard. In this chapter, we explore some ways socialization at home and at school combines with dualistic thinking to contribute to different gender stereotypes or "scripts" for women and men, and we indicate how each of these factors sustains the "tacit assumption" which privileges men's experiences or behaviors and relegates women's to a "subordinate" position in society.

THE INFLUENCE OF DUALISM
ON SHAPING THOUGHT

Much of what has been accepted as "truth" in contemporary society is rooted in a propensity to view the world in terms of opposites. This belief system reflects a legacy that can be traced at least as far back as the sixth century B.C. Lao Tzu in China suggested that change was embodied in the interplay of two poles: "Yin, the condition of darkness, the receptive Earth, the complex intuitive mind, the state of stillness and rest, the female; yang, the condition of light, the creative Heaven, the rational mind, action and motion, the male" (Baxter and Montgomery, 1996, pp. 19–20). From the Pythagorean Brotherhood of the fifth century B.C., dualism has been conceived of as embodied in the following sets of opposites (Wilden, 1987):

Limited/Unlimited
One/Many
Odd/Even
Right/Left
Male/Female
Light/Dark

Looking at the world in bipolar terms shapes both thought and attitudes. For example, one might write a report or a term paper and think "This was easy." But this assessment could be made only if there was prior experience with a similar task that was regarded as "difficult." The terms "easy" and "difficult" and their interpretations are relative. Each is understood in relation to the other. This mutually exclusive, bipolar worldview is limited in a number of ways, as numerous critics and philosophers have established (Cirksana and Cuklanz, 1992).

Three major problems with dualistic thinking have been identified. First, by understanding the world in terms of oppositional qualities we may be led to believe that a concept has *only* two possibilities, and this oversimplification occludes the perception of any middle ground between the terms. Second, as we mentioned above, the paired terms are only "knowable" in relation to each other. So, for example, let us consider the paired terms, "masculine" and "feminine." If one accepts the notion that these two terms inhabit opposite ends of a bipolar spectrum, then one is led to define "feminine" as that which is not "masculine" and vice versa. Neither concept has any meaning on its own, only in relation to what it is not. The third problem with dualist thinking, as philosophers and linguists have established, is that "this dualism generally includes a hierarchical relationship between the terms, valuing one and devaluing the other." (Cirksana and Cuklanz, 1992, p. 20). Men as a class or group frequently have been associated with the relatively more valued term in such bipolar pairs as *mind* and body, *reason* and emotion, *public* and private, *culture* and nature, *subject* and object.

Some trace the initial roots of this division to women's capacity to give birth and men's capacity for physical prowess, coupled with the differential ways those capacities are valued (Bem, 1993; Bernard, 1981; Borisoff and Hahn, 1995a, 1995b; Haste, 1994; Keen, 1991). Embedded in this division is the assumption that women and men have distinct and mutually exclusive functions determined by their biology. Viewing the world in terms of biological differences and using these differences to justify prescribed roles is what Sandra Bem (1993), among others, calls *biological essentialism*. Essentialism is at the core of the gender stereotypes we have discussed in chapter 1. As we have seen, the result of this perspective is that it limits aspirations and is often used to justify discrimination and to keep the "male" and "female" spheres separate.

As we have seen in chapter 1, presumed gender-stereotyped attributes can become the articulated norms of a culture and lead to gender polarization (Bem, 1993). Childhood socialization in the home is one communicative setting in which we will explore the impact of gender-stereotyped behavior. A feature of all known patriarchal cultures is that the public sphere (for example, politics and work outside the home) was initially the exclusive province of men. "Appropriate" communication in this context consequently was predicated on behaviors defined as "masculine." The private sphere (for example, child rearing and work inside the home) was relegated to women. "Appropriate" communication in this context was subsequently based on "feminine" modes of expression. The behavioral modes associated with each sphere have acquired a presumed power that is resistant to challenge or change.

Bem (1993) argues that dividing roles and behaviors according to sex has contributed to and has legitimated *androcentrism* (or male-centeredness). First used by Charlotte Perkins Gilman in *The Man-Made World*, androcentrism is the belief that the experiences and behaviors associated with males are the norm or standard and that those qualities which deviate from this "standard" are consequently devalued. Once behaviors become entrenched, or in the "groove of habit" which Hall calls culture (1981, p. 187), they become "a justification of the dominant group's hegemony" (Blumen, 1994, p. 110).

Although there have been many changes in the decades following Gilman's observations, the tendency to embrace dualistic and androcentric thinking about gender remains pervasive. Such thinking affects expectations for men's and women's communicative behavior. The extent to which socialization and education reinforce the traits and expected roles of women and men merits attention. The following sections examine the impact of these factors on the construction and reinforcement of gender.

SOCIALIZATION: REINFORCING ATTITUDES ABOUT SEX-TRAITS AND SEX-ROLES

Anthropologist Edward T. Hall (1981) has called culture a "silent language" and has explained that cultural norms are learned both directly and indirectly. Gendered behavior is one dimension of culture that is often transmitted indirectly, outside of the conscious awareness of the parties involved.

When a baby is born, the first question asked is, "Is it a boy?" or "Is it a girl?" Jesse Bernard (1981) observes that this question is not benign. Knowing the child's sex will inform every interaction and will determine how the mother, the father, siblings, friends, and how society in general, will respond to the newborn. That single question is the impetus for multiple forces that influence the development of "masculine" and "feminine" traits—traits, moreover, that are intended to direct males and females into separate spheres as adults.

Many parents do not consciously set out to raise their children according to sex stereotypes, yet as much research has established, even unintentional communication between adults and children may reinforce gender stereotypes. Linguist Jean Berko Gleason (1994) studied the impact of sex differences on parent-child interaction. In both home, daycare, and laboratory settings, Gleason examined men and women caregivers interacting with young children. Gleason found that of families studied at home, fathers used twice as many imperatives when speaking with children than did mothers (for example, "Take your plate off the table!" rather than "Would you take your plate off the table, sweetie?"). Fathers also used more sophisticated lexical items and more disparaging terms and threats, particularly when speaking to sons. Greif (1980) found that fathers interrupted their children more than mothers did and that both fathers and mothers interrupted little girls more than little boys. While many parents actively try to resist gender stereotypes in their interactions with children, despite these intentions, studies conducted over the past three decades reveal that familial expectations for masculine and feminine behavior are powerful and may emerge regardless of how gender-neutral parents claim they want the environment to be.

From an early age, little girls are encouraged to demonstrate caring behavior, to form connections with others, to reveal their feelings, and are given toys deemed appropriate for their sex (Bem, 1993; Berman, 1986; Borisoff, 1993; Fagot, 1978; Gilligan, 1982; Graebner, 1982; Haste, 1994; Rubin, 1983; Wood and Inman, 1993). Little boys, in contrast, are encouraged to engage in activities that develop strength and competitiveness. They are expected to monitor and to refrain from revealing feelings that would make them appear vulnerable (Beck, 1988; Bem, 1993; Berman, 1986; Borisoff, 1993; Gerson, 1993; Goleman, 1990; Levant, 1996; Wood and Inman, 1993). Linguist Deborah Cameron (1992) suggests that we need to examine the instrumental, political consequences of such gender-stereotyped child rearing which results in "a dominant identity for males and a subordinate one for females" (p. 76). Although many parents hope that both their sons and daughters will develop into adults who will have personally rewarding occupations and who will share jointly in caring for their future families, Katha Pollitt (1995) suggests that the ways children are raised reflects how tentatively these goals are embraced. Pollitt contends that for many adults "theories of innate differences in behavior are appealing. They let parents off the hook—no small recommendation in a culture that holds moms, and sometimes even dads, responsible for their children's every misstep on the road to bliss and success" (p. 48).

Because it is difficult to resist the cultural forces that guide how children are raised, rigid, dualistic "sex-trait" stereotypes are reinforced and perpetuated. Social psychologists John Williams and Deborah Best define sex-trait stereotypes as "psychological characteristics or behavioral traits that are believed to characterize men with much greater (or lesser) frequency than they characterize women" (1982, p. 16). These researchers claimed that specific characteristics associated with masculinity and femininity are not limited to the United States.

However, even more compelling is research which examines the influential roles culture, socioeconomic class, and ethnicity play in constructing norms of gender and the wide range of different behaviors expected or performed by any given group of men or women. Bonnie Thornton Dill (1996) has established the importance of "making explicit the complex interaction of social and economic forces in shaping the broad historical trends that characterize black women." Dill notes the "pervasiveness" of the image of black women as "economically independent, resourceful, hardworking women" who are "self-reliant, strong [and] autonomous" (pp. 38, 44). Dill attributes the difference between this characterization of black women and the predominant images associated with white, middle-class women to the fact that black women's lives have been characterized by a greater degree of independence from male authority and control and that, "black females have had higher participation rates in the labor force than their white counterparts" (pp. 39–40).

Yet evidently many people continue to associate the category "women" with those qualities assumed to reflect white, middle-class, heterosexual women. In 1995, in an international Gallup Poll surveying one thousand adults in twenty-two countries, "women" were consistently characterized as more "emotional," "talkative," and "affectionate" than men. Men were perceived as more "courageous," "ambitious," and "aggressive" (Lewin, 1996). Taken in isolation these terms have little meaning. However, within the context of specific cultures they speak volumes about attitudes toward and expectations for men and women. These culturally specific gender-differentiated "traits" are reflective of the behaviors children are expected to display as adults, and thus they may become self-fulfilling prophecies. This results in the threat of ostracism and rejection for those men and women who depart from these expected behaviors.

When we begin our lectures on perceptions of gender "differences," many of our students at first assert their beliefs that differences do not exist and that, consequently, avenues for professional development are available equally to women and men. In part to address these students' assumptions, one of the authors surveyed approximately 150 undergraduate students at a private urban university in the early 1990s and repeated the survey in 1997, this time including graduate students. The students were asked to write about how they saw their personal and professional roles in the future. Their responses supported the observation of journalist Susan Faludi (1991), and labor historian Alice Kessler-Harris, of a backlash in attitudes about women and work in the late 1980s. Faludi defines this backlash as "a powerful counterassault on women's rights . . . an attempt to retract the handful of small and hard-won victories that the feminist movement did manage to win for women" (p. xviii). This backlash is evident in the 1995 international Gallup Poll survey in which the majority of respondents in the United States, Chile, Japan, France, and Hungary stated the belief that the "ideal" family structure would be comprised of a father as primary breadwinner and of a mother who stayed home with children (Lewin, 1996).

The majority of the women surveyed in our classes project that their future includes either marriage or involvement in a romantic relationship. There is a qualitative difference, however, in how the undergraduate and graduate students expressed and qualified this prediction. Consistent in the responses of undergraduates was the "hope" or "expectation" that they will be married within five years and will have started to raise a family within ten years. For several of the graduate students, this "hope" was qualified. Some maintained a belief in finding "Mr. Right," "my soulmate," and "someone who will adore me and put me on a pedestal." Yet the majority of this population surveyed wondered whether finding the right person will be possible: "Too many people today get married for all the wrong reasons. I hope I am one of the lucky ones"; "I hope not to be 'pretending' to be happy with the same guy I'm with"; and "I used to think that my life was to be a clone of my parents, but as I get older, I am beginning to realize that it won't necessarily be the case." Such comments reflect a discrepancy between students' earlier expectations and the reality they currently face. These comments, moreover, appeared in responses that cut across ethnic and cultural lines.

Although these responses indicate divergent views on students' prognosis for finding the "right" partner, there was a remarkable consistency in viewing their potential roles as "housewife" and/or "mother" as intrusive dimensions on their professional aspirations. Three patterns emerged in the 1991 study that were echoed in the 1997 responses.

The first pattern indicates that many of the young, predominately middle-class women in these studies viewed their decision to remain in the workforce as an "option" available to them. One 21-year-old female stated: "I would like to pursue a career on Wall Street, become very successful, work for about five to ten years, and then take some time off to raise my children. Ideally, I want my husband to be financially set at this point, so that I don't have to go back to work if I decide that I don't want to." A graduate student similarly projected, "If I have many children, maybe I'll stop working professionally (or just work part-time) and devote my time and energy to my husband, the upbringing of my children, and my home." The model of the nuclear family assumed by both of these students is based on patriarchal notions of male and female responsibility for financial support versus nurturance.

The second pattern that emerged in these self-reported responses relates to the manner in which women who planned to remain in the workforce expected to prioritize their professional and personal lives. Students commented: "In my relationship, being a professional will be second to my role as a woman. I believe being a wife, mother, and partner is more important than my profession"; "The most important thing to me is to make sure whatever career I choose I have time for my family"; and, "I realize that family and work can be difficult to balance, so I am curious to see how my goals turn out." These remarks suggest that, while aware of dichotomous expectations about family and occupational responsibilities, some female students claim they will not allow their careers to interfere with their commitments to their future families. Underlying this assertion, however, is the implicit necessity that, consequently, these women will have to pursue occupations that will make such a balance possible and thus be willing to impose limitations on their professional goals.

The third pattern of student responses revealed a conscious rejection of the traditional roles for women as wife and mother. Many respondents attributed this rejection to their own experiences. Several responses indicated that female students associated the difficulties in their mothers' lives with financial dependency: "I don't want to have to plead with my husband for money the way my mother had to do" and "The power in my family was with my father—he was the breadwinner; he was the professional. I know I am breaking from tradition, but I don't want to be helpless and totally dependent on my husband." For others, the impetus for financial independence emerged from being raised by one parent: "My father died when I was young, and my mother raised us to believe that we have to be able to rely on ourselves. The message was we cannot count on others to support us financially," and "When my dad left, my mother was not prepared to provide for us. She hadn't worked in over fifteen years. Her life became one continuous struggle because her ability to get a good paying job was limited. I will never put myself in that position." These comments suggest that, for many women, the drive for financial independence is rooted in a perception of power inequities. Other responses suggested that middle-class women's professional aspirations were proactive, motivated by a desire for self-definition and social conscience: "I would like to be in a career that is rewarding—enriches the lives of others, and that I enjoy doing" and "Being rich would be nice, but being remembered is my aim." While the majority of the women whose responses fell into this final category expressed the hope that they would marry eventually and have a family, their careers were clearly of prime importance. In several instances, their own financial stability and success would influence their decisions about whether to marry and to start a family. In contrast to those women who view work as an "option" rather than a necessity, these respondents view marriage and parenting as a choice, not a predetermined eventuality.

These patterns tell us something about the lives these specific women hope to forge. The women who depict work outside the home as "optional" or as a secondary concern must, therefore, rely on others, such as their partners, to shoulder the financial obligations. This expectation ignores the fact that most families in the United States are dependent on two incomes for survival. The women whose own experiences taught them not to replicate their mothers' financial dependency view their professional pursuits as protection from becoming dependent on others. The women who regard their professional lives as a form of self-actualization and self-definition seem to envision professional and familial obligations as mutually exclusive. Conspicuously absent in the nearly three hundred responses analyzed were the expression of other, less traditional life choices, such as a vision of heterosexual families with men and women as equal financial partners, with equal responsibility for raising children; families with men as primary caregivers to children while women work outside the home; extended, multi-generational families; or families with gay or lesbian partners.

Like the women students, the men in this study also did not escape the powerful social forces that shape dominant concepts of masculine and feminine behavior. Having a family and career are abiding themes in the men's projections. On the surface, these goals are similar to the women's projections. However, there are marked differences in what family life and professional success signified for the male students when compared with their female peers. Although several of the men envisioned themselves married without children, the majority included having children as part of their future. Distinct from the women's responses, many men stated "I do not see my life changing." While many of the women articulated a need to balance professional goals with their personal lives, the men surveyed did not foresee responsibilities for children as interfering with or impeding their professional aspirations. Implicit in these men's and women's differing responses is that these students have accepted as "inevitable" the essentialized male-as-provider and the woman-as-caretaker roles.

In light of these dichotomous roles, it is not surprising that the men students described "professional success" differently than did the women. Professional and financial success for the women students was often stated within the context of a "rewarding career" or in terms of achieving financial independence as a means to avoid becoming dependent on another. Concern with being dependent on another was virtually absent in the men's responses. For these men, professional success was consistently cast in terms of what money could buy: "I see my wife and I living in a penthouse"; "doing what I want"; "owning a large home." Consistently, professional success was equated with earning power: "I see myself as independently wealthy"; "I will be an extremely successful entrepreneur"; "I will be an executive in the family business." Only one man depicted his future life as a partnership: "Both of us will be working and taking part in organizing a family. I feel that equality is very important in a relationship—to consider your spouse as you would consider yourself."

Largely unexplored by these respondents were options to raise children in extended or collective families, families with gay or lesbian parents, or families where fathers alternate as primary caregivers. While undoubtedly influenced by the backlash against women's active, equal participation in the workforce, attitudes like those expressed by most of these students overlook any awareness of the degree to which the large majority of women are still confined to a "pink-collar ghetto" of low-paying wage labor, while simultaneously assumed to be primarily responsible for a "second shift" of household work when they return home from their jobs. More than fifteen years ago, Lillian Rubin observed that, in popular ideology, the perception is that "Fathers work, mothers 'mother' even when they also work" (1983, p. 175). Men generally see their identities tied to their careers—to the world of work. At the same time, bell hooks (1984) warned against "the romanticization of motherhood" by the media, and she acknowledged a need "to make motherhood neither a compulsory experience for women, nor an exploitative or oppressive one" (p. 136).

Many contemporary women struggle with what sociologist Arlie Russell Hochschild calls "competing urgencies" (1990), to reconcile aspiring to middle-class societal expectations of professional success while maintaining traditional definitions of their roles as wives and mothers. Therefore, when we or our students assume "the naturalness, inevitability, and presumed benefits of marriage," we risk obscuring the power inequities inherent in potentially oppressive binary gender systems. Communication scholar Lana Rakow (1992) has noted we often overlook what historians, anthropologists, and sociologists have established for two decades—that particular "twentieth century Western notions of monogamous, heterosexual marriage are peculiar to this time and place" (as are notions about child rearing in nuclear families). Rakow reminds us that "white definitions of a 'normal' marriage and family" have been used to classify African-American women "as deviant and unfeminine" (pp. 13–14). And bell hooks (1984) suggests that we transform the ways we speak and think about families. "Structured into the definitions and the very usage of the terms 'father' and 'mother' is the sense that the two words refer to two distinctly different experiences. Women and men must define the work of fathering and mothering in the same way if men and women are to accept equal responsibility in parenting" (p. 137).

A study by Kyle Pruett of Yale University supports the contention that fathers who actively participate in raising their children foster healthier gender roles for their sons and daughters. Pruett conducted a longitudinal study on sixteen families from diverse socioeconomic backgrounds where the fathers took primary responsibility for child care while the mothers worked outside of the home full-time. Pruett found that children of both sexes evidenced "masculine" and "feminine" behavior, they were able to play with each other, and they didn't separate into "boy versus girl play." Little boys knew how to care for a baby. According to Pruett, "they didn't see that as a girl's job, they saw it as a human job. I saw the girls have very active images of the outside world and what their mothers were doing in the workplace—things that become interesting to most girls when they're 8 or 10, but these girls were interested when they were 4 or 5" (cited in Shapiro, 1990, p. 65). Thus, whether consciously, or merely by example, multiple role possibilities were communicated to the children.

We have seen how attitudes toward family and career may begin in messages we receive at home. One expectation of the educational process is that it will provide the opportunity for males and females to maximize their potentials in an environment conducive to equality. We turn to an examination of the extent to which opportunity is maximized and equality is achieved.

EDUCATIONAL PRACTICES: A DIFFERENT
EXPERIENCE FOR MALES AND FEMALES

In his book, *The End of Education*, Neil Postman argues that "The schools are, in a word, the affirmative answer to the question, 'Can a coherent, stable, unified culture be created out of people of diverse traditions, languages, and religions?'" (1995, p. 14). By examining the content and process of education, Postman believes that coherence, stability, and unity are possible. These goals are achievable if students are part of a learning environment that provides them with the opportunity to develop the skills, knowledge, values, and attitudes that will help them eventually to find their place in the adult world. Much has been written to suggest, however, that the learning environments for boys and girls are both different and unequal. These differences, moreover, have been directly attributed to gender-based stereotypes (Bem, 1993; Cooper, 1993; Fagot et al., 1985; Fiske, 1990; Markoff, 1989; Powell, 1993; Sadker and Sadker, 1994; Thorne, 1993; Whiting and Edwards, 1988).

Parents expect that their children will be treated fairly by their teachers. The majority of teachers, we would argue, strive to create a learning environment that is inclusive and fair. But teachers, like parents, are products of the culture in which they were raised. Even though they may consciously acknowledge the importance of treating students equally, studies indicate that educators often are unwittingly complicit in reinforcing and perpetuating gender-based (as well as ethnic) stereotypes. Ideas about "sex-trait" and gender stereotypes are sustained in the following ways: through teaching style; through assumptions about student performance; and by not challenging the gender-stereotyped associations of certain disciplines.

Teaching Style

In the mid-1980s, Myra Sadker and David Sadker published a landmark study of how fourth, sixth, and eighth graders receive instruction in mathematics, science, language arts, and English (1984; 1985). After studying more than one hundred classes, these researchers found that "at all grade levels, in all communities and in all subject areas, boys dominated classroom communication. They participated in more interactions than girls did and their participation became greater as the year went on" (1985, p. 56). In reviewing the students' performance, however, what also emerged was that the teachers themselves behaved differently toward the males and females in the classroom. Girls were expected to behave politely and were sanctioned when they attempted to call out answers without raising their hands. The boys, in contrast, were not reprimanded for identical behavior. Moreover, they were given consistent, precise, and positive feedback, while the girls in the same class did not receive the same level of positive reinforcement. The teachers who participated in this study, both male and female, were frequently unaware of the differential messages they were giving their students.

A decade later, the Sadkers contend that schools in the United States are still "failing at fairness" (1994). In their observational studies with elementary school educators, four major discrepancies persist which indicate that the educational experience is different for young girls and young boys. Sadker and Sadker found, for example, that white males continue to receive the majority of the teachers' attention. Minority males, white females, and minority females receive teacher attention in descending order with minority females receiving the least amount. Attention paid to students has been found to correlate positively with both achievement and self-esteem. The lack of attention paid especially to minority females may offer further explanation for earlier findings by Jacqueline Jordan Irvine. Irvine's research (1986) determined that as young women of color progress through elementary school, their initial involvement in classroom-related activities diminishes over time.

A second finding reveals that, over time, the learning climate remains unequal for young boys and girls. As they progress through school, boys continue to receive from teachers the three kinds of feedback that promote problem-solving and critical thinking skills: praise, remediation, and criticism. Girls, in contrast, receive more acceptance responses, the type of message "that packs far less educational punch" (Sadker and Sadker, 1994, p. 54), since it does not further their learning process. Moreover, teachers afford male students a longer response time to arrive at answers. The implicit message children receive is that boys *should* speak up and out in the classroom. As a result of this type of encouragement, which reinforces the gender stereotypes we identified in chapter 1, male students learn to dominate class discussion. This behavior is evident at all levels, including college (Keegan, 1989; Pearson and West, 1991). This process, Sandler (1991) suggests, may undermine women's self-confidence over time and limit professional aspirations.

Physical appearance is the one trait for which teachers provide more feedback to young girls. The teachers Sadker and Sadker interviewed indicated that complimenting a girl (i.e., telling her how pretty her new dress is, how attractive her new haircut is, and so on), was a form of "connecting" with the child. As one teacher commented, "They look so happy when you tell them they're pretty. . . . I think it's what they're used to hearing, the way they are rewarded at home" (Sadker and Sadker, 1994, p. 56). According to numerous researchers who have studied physical appearance, beauty as a cultural imperative for females is learned at a very young age. Although both sexes are concerned with social acceptance for their appearance, for young girls social estimations of "attractiveness" are linked directly with their physical appearance, whereas for young boys "attractiveness" includes other traits such as being good at sports (Freedman, 1986; Tarvis, 1992; Wolf, 1991). When teachers draw attention to and compliment a girl's physical attractiveness, although they may regard their remarks as a form of bonding, they are simultaneously reinforcing the centrality of appearance to female identity. These messages, Borisoff and Hahn contend, may have far-reaching implications:

> They are perpetuating a valuation of body image as intimately connected to self-esteem, self-worth, and future success. Being "daddy's little angel" also connotes that the little girl will always be taken care of. The connection between beauty and dependence is obvious. If a good little girl conforms to the prescription to be pretty, cute—that is feminine—she can depend on (or be dependent on) a man to care for her in later life. Thus, appearance, dependency, and security become inexorably linked for the female child. (1997b, p. 103)

How young girls and boys negotiate, appropriate, and value space is the fourth area revealed in the Sadkers' study. When boys engage in team sports on the playground and the girls are clustered together on the periphery, or when they eat in sex-segregated groups in the lunchroom, or when boys chase or tease the girls, many teachers accept the division of space and the behavior as "normal." Ostensibly the students are getting along; however, frequently they are getting along in separate spheres. Sociologist Barrie Thorne (1993) has examined the "landscape of contemporary childhood" within schools and found that implicit in this early separation is that boys control space; if left unchallenged, this separation increases as the children get older. Thorne suggests that spatial gender boundaries are constructed and maintained in classroom activities that pit the boys against the girls and that these gender "borders" while not impermeable, "feed an assumption of gender as dichotomous and antagonistic difference" (p. 87)—a difference that is shaped by male dominance. As with appearance, how boys and girls learn to negotiate and control space often begins in the home. According to Gill Valentine, "studies have found that boys are allowed to range further from home unsupervised and to spend more time outdoors than girls . . . this gender difference in children's geographies is a product of parents' greater concern for daughters' safety and the fact that girls' activities are more constrained because they have more responsibilities in the home than boys" (1997, p. 39).

Although some claim that the perception of young girls' greater vulnerability may be the initial impetus to create different spheres for males and females, in the educational environment, spatial differences are perpetuated not to protect young girls, but to exclude them. "It is the boys," the Sadkers contend, "who work hardest at raising the walls of sex segregation and intensifying the difference between the genders" (1994, p. 62). When boys resort to chasing, teasing, and touching to protect their territory from being "invaded" by the girls and when teachers accept this behavior as "a harmless bigotry" (Sadker and Sadker, 1994, p. 220), they are contributing to the view that females are not merely different but "opposite" and ultimately less valued, since it is the *girls* who are restricted and not the boys who chase them. Without "intervention by adults who can equalize the playing field," little girls may never learn to question "this hidden curriculum in second-class citizenship" (Sadker and Sadker, 1994, p. 62).

Assumptions about Student Performance

Although girls' and boys' potential for academic learning is equal, several studies suggest that *expectations* for academic achievement exert a potent influence on the extent to which a child's potential is fulfilled. While meta-analytic studies of students' verbal and mathematical performances have indicated that differences between the scores of males and females have declined (Hyde, Fennemo, and Lamon, 1990; Hyde and Linn, 1988), a 1990 survey of three thousand children, sponsored by the American Association of University Women, revealed a disturbing trend. From fourth to tenth grade, the percentage of girls who said they were "happy the way I am" dropped from 60 to 29 percent; for boys the figure dropped from 67 to 46 percent. African-American girls maintained more self-confidence than white girls. Thorne (1993) notes that "compared with boys of the same age, and with themselves at earlier ages, girls who are twelve, thirteen, and four-teen have higher rates of depression, lower self-esteem, more negative images of their own bodies, and declining academic performance in areas like math and science" (p. 155). To what can we attribute this change in girls' self-perception? Is there a relationship between this and the messages girls receive about their talents, their bodies, and their intellectual abilities?

When adults were asked to picture an "intellectual" child, Raty and Snellman (1992) found that 57 percent of the female respondents and 71 percent of the male respondents in their study depicted male children. When high school students were asked to draw a "scientist," 100 percent of the boys and 84 percent of the girls drew a man (Sadker and Sadker, 1994). Collis and Ollila (1990) report a positive correlation between associating academic subjects with gender and male and female students' respective attitudes and performance in these subjects. Many people consider language, writing, and literature to be "feminine" subjects, since they are associated with expressiveness and creativity; science and math are viewed as "masculine" subjects, since they are associated with logic and "proof" claims. We ought not be surprised that such views influence students' performance, selections of fields of study, and ultimately careers (Bem, 1993; Cooper, 1993; Jamieson, 1995; Sadker and Sadker, 1994). Yet since biological differences do not account for associating science, mathematics, and intellectual rigor with boys and men, how can we explain the prevalence of these associations? Studies indicate that for many these attitudes develop in the home and are reinforced in the classroom.

As with appearance and use of space, parents' and caregivers' messages play a significant role in how their children perform mathematically. According to Jacquelynne Eccles and Janis Jacobs (1986), mothers' views on the relevance of math courses and their own anxieties about the subject's difficulty are often transmitted to their children. If a woman has experienced difficulty in her own background with mathematics, she may convey her anxiety to her son and daughter. However, if she embraces the perception that mathematics is "an appropriate activity for males . . . (and is) a male domain" (Pedro et al., 1981, p. 208), her son is likely to receive more encouragement to succeed in this area than her daughter. Fathers' attitudes also appear to have a major influence on their daughters' mathematical development (Fennema and Sherman, 1977). Fennema and Sherman specifically note a correlation between fathers' general attitudes toward gender roles and their daughters' mathematical performances.

Teachers' beliefs about "gender-appropriate" subjects similarly influence whether the classroom climate in a given subject area is receptive or "chilly" for students. In 1990, Gail Jones and Jack Wheatley published a study based on their observations of thirty chemistry and thirty physical science classes. They found male students to be more assertive than female students in class. Their findings, like those of the Sadkers, also revealed that the female students received less praise and encouragement. When students perceive that they are not welcome in a classroom, they may cope by becoming more passive (Rosenfeld and Jarrard, 1986); or they may cope by dropping out (Sadker and Sadker, 1994). In addition, students may have internalized a fear of success if they are penalized or ridiculed by peers or teachers when they demonstrate skills in areas not traditionally associated with their gender. For example, if our culture and our classrooms conspire by accepting that "girls are supposed to be less good at math" (Shapiro, 1990, p. 57), we ought not be surprised that this message will be internalized. If parents convey the belief that a particular subject has limited relevance to their child's own life, and if educators create a learning environment that marginalizes the presence of girls and women, these messages will become associated with the discipline.

When technology entered the classroom it was hoped that the utilization of computers would level the academic playing field for male and female students. It is now imperative that all education environments encourage computer competency and literacy. In virtually every subject area, rapidly changing technology has the potential to reshape the parameters of a given discipline. However, three-fourths of the children enrolled in computer camps are males (Markoff, 1989), 60 percent of the male students in the United States compared with approximately 20 percent of the female students enter schools with prior at-home instruction in computers (Sadker and Sadker, 1994), and computer courses are housed in departments of mathematics (Sanders, 1984). Thus, it is not surprising that young children view computer use as masculine (Collis and Ollila, 1990) and that female students regard computer training as optional (Hoyles, 1988) and are thereby discouraged from developing the comfort and expertise with technology that will be an increasingly vital part of their educational environment.

Yet, female students' attitudes toward math, science, and computers have changed when concerted efforts are made to expose them to women professionals in fields that are still associated with men and when pro-active measures are adopted to diminish gender-bias in the classroom (Fish, Gross, and Sanders, 1986; Martinez, 1992; Peltz, 1990). At this point in time, however, more sustained and pervasive efforts are needed to discourage female students from selecting out of those areas of study that may limit their academic future as well as their professional opportunities. It is important, moreover, for educators to acknowledge the conflicting messages girls and boys receive in the classroom and to realize that sustaining differences in academic performance can affect significantly how each child will develop as an adult both in the workplace and in her or his personal relationships.

Suggested Activities

A. Focus on Sex-Role Expectations

1. Write briefly about how you envision your personal and professional life in the next five to ten years. (You may also obtain this information about your peers by interviewing several students or colleagues.) The class may then be divided into groups; the participants discuss the responses. The following may be discussed with the entire group:

   a. Did the group share goals and attitudes about the future?

   b. Were similar goals and attitudes shared by women? by men?

   c. Do the expressed goals reflect stereotyped gender expectations?

2. Complete the following: "I wish my parents would have allowed or encouraged me to be more _____ ." Working in groups, consider the extent to which this "wish" conforms to or deviates from the "sex-trait" stereotypes posited by Williams and Best.

B. Focus on Valuing Gendered Socialization

The following questions will be posed to class members: *To the women*—was there ever a point when you were younger that you wanted to be a boy? *To the men*—at some point in your life, did you want to be a girl? (Research has indicated that women typically wanted to be a male; men, in contrast almost never claim to having wanted to be a female.) How does the relative social devaluation of women influence attitudes?

C. Focus on Sex-Role and Sex-Trait Stereotypes in Education

1. In her study of children's books that had received the Caldecott Medal or the Newberry Award, Pamela Cooper found that gen-

der stereotyping of the adult figures in these books has persisted over nearly two-and-a-half decades (1993, p. 125). Either in groups or individually, examine current award-winning children's books and assess the extent to which gender, ethnicity, and class stereotypes persist and how such stereotypes are interconnected.

2. Students will divide into groups of 5 or 6. Each group member should recall his/her least favorite and most favorite academic subject. This recollection should include how he/she viewed teachers or professors. Discuss the extent to which any patterns occur that may be attributed to gender and how these previous experiences may have shaped each person's current major or career.

Chapter Five

Gendered Scripts
Women and Men in the Workplace

> But, you may say, we asked you to speak about women and fiction—what
> has that got to do with a room of one's own? I will try to explain. . . . All I
> could do was to offer you an opinion upon one minor point—a woman
> must have money and a room of her own if she is to write fiction: and that,
> as you will see, leaves the great problem of woman and the true nature of
> fiction unsolved.
>
> — Virginia Woolf, "A Room of One's Own"

What is striking about the above-cited quotation is its simplicity. For
the artist to write, she must have a place to call her own; she must have
a roof over her head. In early twentieth-century England, men's economic dominance was, in Woolf's view, a major barrier to women's
artistic achievement and the root of other problems for women as well.
According to Woolf scholar Mitchell A. Leaska, "A Room of One's Own"
has become, "the classic essay on feminism" (1984, p. 168).

Women's need for economic autonomy has been an abiding concern for centuries. As historian Phyllis Stock-Morton (1991) noted, "for
any cohort of women born in Europe after the fifteenth century, 10–
20% remained single; and at any time one quarter to one half of all
women under thirty were unmarried" (p. 63). Yet the predominant
middle-class ideology that cast men exclusively as "breadwinners" and
women as their "dependents"—whether or not they had to labor for
their own sustenance—has continued to shape the experiences of
working women and men.

Although many changes resulting in decreased economic dominance of males over females have occurred since Woolf's essay,

numerous barriers persist. Many women now "own their own room"; however, the rooms they own are different and smaller than the rooms owned by men. Drawing on diverse fields that include communication, history, psychology, sociology, and the mass media, we examine six major factors that sustain gender stereotypes in the workplace.

GENDER STEREOTYPING: MAINTAINING THE MYTH OF "WOMEN'S WORK" AND "MEN'S WORK"

Despite the large percentage of women in the United States workforce, many reports indicate that women and men are still not treated equally. While some studies examine how far women have come, others look at how far we still need to go in order to achieve equality for women in the workplace. There are articles in the popular press that herald the "Best News Ever for Women" (Allen, 1993), "The Feminization of Management" (Lee, 1994), and claim that women as managers are "Not Just Different—[but] Better" (Collingwood, 1995). Other articles address "The Truth About Women's Pay" (Mahar, 1993), deliver the "Somber News for Women on [the] Corporate Ladder" (Dobrzynski, 1996), and maintain that "Women and Minorities Still Face [the] Glass Ceiling" (Kilborn, 1995). Thus the "meaning" of gender differences in the workplace depends upon the perspective from which the data is examined.

According to U.S. government statistics, nearly 90 percent of men and 70 percent of women between the ages of twenty and fifty-four are in the labor force (U.S. Department of Labor, 1989). Yet as of 1989, nearly 75 percent of full-time working women earned less than $20,000 a year (Newton, 1989, p. 268). Although the doors to employment may be open to women, career aspirations and expectations are shaped in part by what individuals *perceive as possible*. What individuals regard as possible is influenced by how they see themselves within the larger society of which they are a member and these self-perceptions are shaped by the messages and discourse systems to which they are exposed.

Herbert Blumer (1969) viewed this perceptual process as one aspect of the construction of the "self," that is, who we become is influenced by how others see us and define us. What is expected of us informs what we may come to expect for ourselves. As African-American feminist theorist bell hooks (1984) explained, "women are exploited economically in jobs but they are also exploited psychologically. They are taught via sexist ideology to devalue their contributions to the labor force" (p. 101). Hooks notes the need to "attribute value to all work women do, whether paid or unpaid," and warns against the practice of some middle-class white "women's liberationists" (as she called them) to equate careerism and class mobility with liberation. She points out that the majority of African-American women and working-class white women have worked outside the home for centuries, "working in jobs that neither liberated them from dependence on men, nor made them economically self-sufficient" (p. 95). Hooks implores us to rethink the nature of work and reminds us that race, class, and gender are interconnected in our experiences in the workplace, as they are in all other contexts.

Think back to the primarily middle-class gender stereotypes we identified in chapter 1. Undergirding these archetypical depictions of "femininity" was an association with domesticity—an association that is still operative in many workplaces. For example, certain jobs such as nursing, elementary teaching, and clerical and administrative support positions are still largely viewed as "women's work." Other, more prestigious and higher-paying jobs are conventionally regarded as "men's work" (for example, engineering, mathematics, computer science, law, and medicine) despite the fact that the practitioner's sex is irrelevant in fulfilling her or his occupational responsibilities (Roberts, 1995). In fact, some fields, such as health care, are or had been traditionally female-dominated in some cultures and historical periods and only became male-dominated when a formal, institutionalized authorizing body, such as the American Medical Association, decided to impose training and licensing requirements which women were prohibited from meeting. Thus, by the nineteenth century, most female midwives and healers were replaced by male doctors.

Whether intentionally or inadvertently, gender-dichotomous occupational expectations may be supported by families who want their children to fit in with dominant societal expectations. Similarly, educators, cognizant of typical career paths for men and women, pressure children to conform with and to accept unquestioningly the career opportunities associated with each sex. As of 1992, 90 percent of all nursing positions, 75 percent of all kindergarten-through-twelfth-grade teaching positions, and 80 percent of all administrative support (including clerical) positions were held by women, whereas only 9 percent of engineering positions, 27 percent of legal positions, and 22 percent of medical positions were held by women respectively (Roberts, 1995; U. S. Department of Labor, 1992).

According to Gary Powell (1993) children become aware of these "professional ghettos" at an early age (p. 69). They also learn to value gender-stereotyped work differentially. Margaret Mooney Marini and Mary Brinton (1984) reported that while 35 percent of the women in their study ages fourteen to twenty-two aspired to "male-identified" occupations, only 4 percent of the men aspired to occupations that were identified as "female-intensive" (cited in Powell, 1993, p. 76).

Perhaps as a result of these cultural messages, since 1970 many women have entered occupations traditionally defined as "masculine" (Roberts, 1995). During a twenty-year period, there has been a significant increase in the percentages of women moving into these fields (for example, from 14 to 44 percent in economics, from 6 to 27 percent in the legal field, from 11 to 29 percent in medicine, and from 17 to 29 percent in chemistry) (Roberts, 1995). Some researchers have associated the increase of women in traditionally male-dominated fields with influences provided by: changing familial role models, such as mothers working outside the home; highly educated parents; and parents' attitudes about their daughters' careers (Powell, 1993; Sandberg et al., 1987). However, general language use continues to reflect prevalent stereotypical attitudes about gender in the workplace. For example, women's choices to pursue a wider range of occupations are described as pursuing "atypical careers" or "nontraditional fields"; "scaling" occupational walls; and "breaking through glass ceilings" which constrain women from access to the most powerful and lucrative careers.

Hiring Practices: How Appearances Are "Read" by Employers

Gender stereotypes not only affect individuals' career decisions but also influence who is hired. Studies conducted during the 1980s and 1990s reveal that from entry to exit, women are typically treated differently than their male colleagues. Even before they enter the workplace, according to McIntyre, Mohberg, and Posner (1980), women experience discrimination. In their study on responses to unsolicited resumes, these researchers found that women were less likely than men to receive responses from companies. Furthermore, Heilman's (1984) study on sex bias in work settings suggests that in the absence of other concrete information, individuals tend to rely on stereotypes. Thus, even before a candidate arrives in person, gender stereotypes in the mind of the interviewer may already have been engaged.

Meeting a job applicant does not diminish the effects of gender stereotyping. Numerous researchers have determined that appearance affects hiring decisions (Eagly et al., 1991; Heilman, 1984; Knapp and Hall, 1997; Powell, 1993). Unless totally irrelevant to a particular job, perceptions of physical attractiveness affect hiring practices. According to Eagly et al., (1991), "beauty" has been equated with social competence. Thus, an applicant's appearance "may be an advantage in obtaining a job, obtaining a more prestigious job, and being hired at a larger salary" even over a "less attractive competitor [who] is more qualified for the position" (Knapp and Hall, 1997, p. 204). Yet, as we have seen in the previous chapter, when considering the deleterious impact of focusing on a girl's appearance in the educational environment, the conflation of concerns about workplace performance and a worker's appearance is clearly problematic for a number of reasons. First, the concept of "attractiveness" is culturally influenced. In addition to gender stereotypes, racist, classist, ethnocentrist, and heterosexist stereotypes are imbricated in any notion of "attractiveness." Second, the objectification of women reinforces stereotyped notions about attractiveness and gendered behavior, since traditional white, middle-class markers of "attractiveness" are often equated with dominant conceptions of "femininity." It is important to remember that "attractiveness" is not deemed essential for men's advancement (Knapp and Hall, 1997, p. 204). Third, the socially constructed concept of femininity does not coincide with the "masculine" paradigm operative in many workplaces. Thus, employers may subconsciously anticipate that stereotypically "feminine" women would not perform well in certain managerial or "nontraditional" careers.

The culture of every organization contains implicit norms for its members' appearance. As we have seen in chapter 3, dress is a form of artifactual communication, and this may also influence hiring decisions. Several studies indicate that women, in particular, are judged by how they dress for interviews (Davis, 1992; Forsythe, 1990; Forsythe, Drake, and Cox, 1985; Hughes, 1987). Certainly men are also judged by their appearance. However, Fred Davis (1992) contends that business attire was fashioned by men, for men. "Professional attire" has come to be equated with masculine vestimentary norms that place women in a double bind. Clothing, like language, is a symbol which can be read as a mark of "in-group" belonging, or fitting in. The double bind faced by women applying for professional positions lies in finding how to communicate their "in-group" status without dressing in a manner regarded as "too masculine," which could result in negative hiring decisions based upon gender stereotyped or homophobic interpretations of the woman's display of gender. On the other hand, "too feminine" apparel would be considered too frivolous for the workplace. This is further complicated because women are encouraged to construct and display a "style" as if this were reflective of their personality and for which they will be judged. Dress is actually an arena wherein individuals communicate the ways in which they want to present themselves and be seen in the workplace.

A final factor affecting hiring decisions is employers' bias. Despite ethical and legal constraints, organizations may make hiring decisions based on the perception that it would be "uncomfortable" to deal with an applicant because of her/his sex, ethnicity, or religion. Epstein's (1981) study of law firms revealed that often women were not hired because the hiring attorneys claimed that clients would not be as comfortable dealing with a woman as they would with a man. Women are frequently not selected for international management positions because employers assumed that they will encounter prejudice abroad (Adler, 1994). Even when they are hired, women often find that they are not afforded the opportunity to participate fully. In a 1990 national poll more than 80 percent of chief executives at Fortune 1000 companies acknowledged that discrimination impeded female employees' progress—yet less than 1 percent of these same companies regarded *remedying* sex discrimination as a goal that their personnel departments should pursue (Faludi, 1991, pp. xiii–xiv). Diana Henrique describes the message inherent in one organization's practice of providing a male-only party for Japanese visitors: "It was deemed important that the Japanese visitors be put at ease, that they feel at home. And at home is where the women in their lives traditionally stay. So their ever-so-tactful New York hosts apparently decided that their women—wives and executives—should stay home too" (1989, p. 1).

Despite the overt biases that many women confront, Powell (1993) projects a brighter picture for women entering the business world. He contends that an applicant's qualifications, communication ability, prior experience, initiative, and knowledge of the job being applied for are the most salient factors in making hiring decisions (Graves and Powell, 1988). While we may question the grounds for this degree of optimism, given the studies and statistics cited above, interviewers do appear less likely to rely on gender-based stereotypes when they have access to sufficient information about and can meet with prospective employees. However, bias need not be intentional to have occurred.

SALARY PRACTICES:
MAINTAINING ECONOMIC DISPARITIES

Once hired, studies indicate that women do not fare as well as men in the workplace. According to the United States Census Bureau, in 1988 women with a college diploma earned 59 cents to their male counterparts' dollar, a pay gap as far behind a man's salary as women experienced two decades earlier (U.S. Department of Labor, Feb. 1989, table 35). We look at four factors that may contribute to this difference: differing expectations about salary; different opportunities for mentoring; expectations about gendered career paths and child-care considerations; and discrimination against women which results in occupations associated with women being valued less than those associated with men.

First, in a series of studies examining women's reactions to earning less than men in comparable positions, Brenda Major (1987) found that women had lower career-entry and career-peak salary *expectations* than men had (p. 139). Moreover, Major reported that women dealt with salary disparities by comparing their expectations with those of other women, rather than men. Only by raising women's awareness about inequities and inequalities in the professional compensation and reward system can women begin to change their own notions of entitlement. In the author's words, "For women to recognize the degree to which they are victimized and undervalued in society and by its agents entails psychic costs. So, too, however, does blaming oneself rather than the system for failing to obtain desired rewards" (Major, 1987, p. 145).

Second, the wage differential has been connected to *discrimination* against women. A bipartisan federal commission reported a significant gap in the mean income of white males as compared to the earnings of men and women of color and white women. These findings appeared in selected industries in the private sector including business services, manufacturing companies, retail companies, and the transportation industry (Kilborn, 1995). *Even when comparable experience was taken into account, men's incomes exceeded those of women.* The commission suggested that the wage gap is exacerbated in part because "women and minority groups (of both sexes) are not receiving the close mentoring and other support that white men automatically receive from other white men" (Kilborn, 1995, p. C22). According to Maggie Mahar (1993), this lack of mentoring and support affects women in many disciplines and may explain, in part, why women in the medical field "are usually pediatricians and diagnosticians, not surgeons," why in the legal field women "are far more likely to specialize in taxes and trusts and estates, and are far less likely to be groomed to be star litigators," and why on Wall Street women "are frequently the analysts, writing the reports that tell better-paid managers how to invest'" (p. 100). The discrimination that has kept women out of the highest ranks of professional employment has resulted in women comprising less than 8 percent of all federal and state judges, less than 6 percent of all law partners, and less than half of 1 percent of top corporate managers (Faludi, 1991, p. xiii).

Cox and Blake's (1991) study on managing cultural diversity suggests that even when organizations hire members of diverse groups, often they fail to address quality-of-work-life issues that would promote assimilation and facilitate professional advancement for their employees. Only when organizations are truly proactive in embracing and valuing a diverse workforce will each employee receive the type of training and encouragement necessary for professional mobility (Cox and Blake, 1991).

Leaves of absence from the workplace—especially for child care—is the third factor that leads to wage disparities between what women and men earn. According to Joy Schneer of Rider University's College of Business Administration, "The traditional managerial career path of a continued uninterrupted climb up the corporate ladder is still held in high regard. If you violate that, there are repercussions" (cited in Jacobs, 1994, p. 1). When workers—overwhelmingly women—who are also assumed to be primarily responsible for the care of children, or aging parents, are punished professionally for taking time away from their work lives to provide such care, they are subject to an androcentric perspective in which the work and the home environments are considered two separate and mutually exclusive spheres. The impact of child care on one's career will be examined more fully later in this chapter.

The final factor that contributes to different salaries for women and men is linked to social *devaluation* of jobs associated with women when compared to those associated with men. Just as we saw, in chapter 2 how the linguistic practices that signify "femininity" have been regarded less desirable than those believed to signal "masculine" usage, so too, gender disparate professional opportunities and choices receive differential status and remuneration. In their study on compensation differentials, sociologists Jerry Jacobs and Ronnie Steinberg (1995) suggest a possible connection between the perception of "extreme" working conditions, such as stress coupled with hazardous or undesirable tasks, and compensation. Their findings suggest that these extreme conditions are *presumed* to be more prevalent in male-dominated jobs, which would contribute to a wage gap. But as the 1984–85 court case between the Equal Employment Opportunity Commission and Sears, Roebuck & Company illustrated, hiring procedures that "protected" women from the "rough and tumble world of commission sales" could be justified by an appeal to gender stereotypes, by claiming that saleswomen "preferred" lower paying salesclerk jobs, rather than more "strenuous" jobs of selling appliances, for example (Faludi, 1991, pp. 378–88).

Because women historically have had neither the economic nor the political power of (self-)definition to establish the parameters for evaluating and valuing jobs, both the attributes of the jobs they held as well as the skills they brought to the workplace have often been rendered invisible (Bem, 1993; Bernard, 1981; Steinberg, 1990; Stockard and Johnson, 1980). Without the power to accurately name one's condition, as Jacobs and Steinberg (1995, p. 116) contend, a "lack of recognition of the characteristics differentially found in 'historically female' jobs extends to the undesirable working conditions found in these jobs. These working conditions are often not captured in the standard surveys of work attributes" thereby making it more difficult for women to make a case for additional compensation. Thus the nurse, whose job brings her into contact with blood, infectious diseases, and human waste may have greater difficulty making a case for higher wages than the sanitation worker whose work brings him into contact with potentially disease-producing waste. The "dirt" they deal with, Remick (1984) claims, is perceived differently.

Professions associated with women and with "feminine" qualities such as caregiving, nurturance, and expressiveness have been typically underrepresented in powerful unions as well as "in the wage-setting echelons of corporate decision-making." These stereotypes, whereby occupational fields are "tainted" by being female-dominant, coupled with the biases that cast employees who are members of marginalized groups as "less committed" and more "easily replaceable" than white male employees, may account for the persistence of disparities in wages (Jacobs and Steinberg, 1995, pp. 118–19).

GENDER IN THE WORKPLACE: QUESTIONING DIFFERENCES IN PROFESSIONAL PERFORMANCE

According to Sue DeWine (1987, p. 19), organizational culture can be defined as a set of expected behaviors that are generally supported within the group. This set of expectations or norms usually consists of unwritten "rules" that have an immense impact on behavior. Recent studies have attempted to identify behaviors associated with effective leadership. Drawing on work by Bredin (1995), Collingwood (1995), Eagly and Johnson (1990), Eagly and Karau (1991), Hymowitz and Schellhardt (1986), Lee (1994), Morrison, White, and Van Velsor, (1992), Powell (1993), Wilkins and Anderson (1991), as well as from our own consultancies with organizations, we summarize below the attributes and behaviors that signify effective leadership and discuss the relationship between these communicative acts and gender stereotypes.

Behaviors Associated with Effective Management

Personal Characteristics:

1. high self-confidence
2. high motivation to manage
3. high need for self-actualization
4. accessible to others
5. nonjudgmental of others
6. able to manage stress
7. effective networker
8. inspires trust
9. decisive
10. sensitive to diversity issues
11. shows interest & concern for others

Professional Qualities:

1. embraces organization's values
2. expresses a team orientation
3. has an open-door policy
5. delegates responsibility
4. maximizes employee potential
6. facilitates change
7. highly effective
8. creates inclusive environment
9. highly competent
10. fosters cooperation
11. democratic approach
12. is consistent
13. effective problem solver
14. creates collegial atmosphere

Communication Behaviors That Reflect
Personal and Professional Traits:

1. listens willingly and effectively
2. provides positive feedback
3. offers constructive criticism
4. encourages equal communication
5. conveys empathy
6. nonverbal and verbal behaviors are congruent

The qualities listed in the summary above reflect a transition that has occurred in cultural values. Riane Eisler (1987, p. 206) describes it as a transformation from an exclusively hierarchical system based on a "dominator" model of effective organizational communication to a "partnership" model which stresses cooperation and collaboration. As you can see, this current model draws upon behaviors traditionally associated with both men and women. Organizational behaviors associated with effective management which reflect stereotypical "feminine" communicative styles include accessibility, sensitivity, concern for others, cooperation, team orientation, inclusivity, listening, and empathy. Qualities traditionally associated with masculine stereotypes include decisiveness, self-confidence, and motivation to manage others. The researchers contend that success in organizational settings depends upon performing a wide repertoire of behaviors that transcends either stereotype.

Fortunately, for many, incorporating a blend of behaviors appears to be the management style of choice. Numerous studies have demonstrated a positive correlation between the increasing number of women in collegial positions with men and an increase in men's use of supportive statements (Aries, 1987; Bohn and Stutman, 1983); a decrease in argumentativeness and combativeness (Piliavin and Martin, 1978); and a decline in the likelihood of men ascribing gender-based stereotypes to their female colleagues (Bass, Krusell, and Alexander, 1971; Eagly and Karau, 1991). There is strong historical precedent for anticipating a positive impact as a result of women's and men's employment in the same occupations. Elinor Lerner's (1986) study of family structure, occupation patterns, and support for women's suffrage among working men and immigrants in New York City in the first two decades of the twentieth century found a positive correlation between ethnicity, occupation, and support or lack of support for women's right to vote. In areas where support for women's suffrage was highest, women were twice as likely to work, three times as likely to be working wives, and four times as likely to be working mothers than in antisuffrage neighborhoods. Interestingly, male voters' support for women's right to vote was highest among Jewish men who worked side-by-side with women in the garment industry and lowest among Irish men who were primarily employed in sex-segregated fields as laborers, teamsters, and longshoremen. We speculate that the opportunity to communicate and work alongside women in a unionized trade where both men and women were identified as "workers" was influential in men's support for women's rights.

Many studies of contemporary professional men and women report minimal differences and greater overlap in their behaviors. Harlan and Weiss (1982), for example, studied one hundred managers (fifty males, fifty females) from two major companies and discovered more psychological similarities than differences: "Men and women were found to have very similar psychological profiles of high power and achievement needs, high self-esteem, and high motivation to manage" (p. 91). Similarities have also been found in the ways male and female managers express themselves in such areas as affective behavior, influence tactics, autocratic versus democratic behaviors, and facilitative communication (Wilkins and Andersen, 1991). Watson's (1994) review of studies published since 1975 found women and men negotiators similarly competitive; perceived *power and status* rather than *gender* were determined to be more significant in influencing negotiator style.

Many professional women are adept at demonstrating behaviors traditionally associated with masculine stereotypes, therefore one may speculate that only those women who choose to exhibit these traits are drawn to, retained, and promoted within the ranks of professions still regarded as male bastions. As with the specific verbal and nonverbal behaviors we discussed in chapters 2 and 3, some researchers contend that, overall, women's and men's communication styles in the workplace, as well as in personal interaction, may be more similar than different (Canary and Hause, 1993; Coates, 1986; Dindia and Allen, 1992; Inman, 1996). Others speculate that women may intentionally develop behaviors associated with the traditional masculine stereotype in order to compete in the workplace, cognizant that these behaviors deviate from those they were raised to enact. Those who believe that women and men were socialized to value distinct (and often unequal) spheres embrace a "dual culture" approach to studying gender (Bem, 1993; Haste, 1994; Johnson, 1989; Tannen, 1990, 1994).

While the "dual culture" approach acknowledges that women in the workplace often are placed in a double bind of having to behave in ways construed as neither "too masculine" nor "too feminine" (Jamieson, 1995; Putnam, 1983), this theory has been used, on occasion, to *reinforce* the limiting dualistic approach to gender we described in the previous chapter. Despite those who claim that women's and men's workplace behaviors are the result of mutually exclusive enculturation, a survey of 1,460 managers by the American Management Association found no significant differences in women's and men's managerial styles and professional commitment. In fact, these surveys reported that women managers were more likely than men to relocate for promotions and "in conflicts between important home and business responsibilities, [executive women were] more likely to favor their jobs" (Hymowitz and Schellhardt, 1986, p. 5D).

Despite the similarities in professional performance by women and men, continuing stereotyped *perceptions about* women professionals suggest that organizations may be paying lip service to, rather than embracing, gender diversity in the workplace. These perceptions impede women's success. The *Wall Street Journal* reported that although there has been a steady increase in women entering the managerial ranks, it will take a full two to three decades for women to achieve parity with men (Lee, 1994). A recent Catalyst survey reports that women still hold only 2 percent of the power positions in the five hundred largest companies in the United States (Dobrzynski, 1996). There are several possible causes for this enormous disparity.

As we suggested in the previous chapter, the propensity to dichotomize the domains of work and home according to gender may explain why many people continue to regard stereotypical "masculine" traits as appropriate for managers and why men persist in describing successful managers as men, despite the positive impact of adopting the qualities of effective management we presented earlier (Bem, 1993; Borisoff and Hahn, 1995b; Epstein, 1991; Morrison, White, and Van Velsor, 1992; Powell, 1993). Moreover, as long as "the upper levels of management remain a male bastion"—in other words, as long as it serves the interests of those in power to maintain the status quo—the stereotypes may remain the same (Powell, 1993, p. 156).

According to Mary Mattis, vice-president of research and advisory services at Catalyst, the belief that women are "more supportive, better team players," may lead to an association with "staff and support positions" rather than with positions that require tough decision making and risk taking (cited in Lee, 1994, p. 29). Thus, according to Stewart (1982) the task assignments given to women may differ from those given to men, thereby preventing women from engaging in those experiences that could lead to promotion. A Catalyst survey of CEOs and senior human resource executives confirmed that these assumptions are "the most important factor in maintaining the glass ceiling that keeps women out of top jobs" (Lee, 1994, p. 29).

Women encounter two additional barriers which they share with members of minority groups of both sexes in the workplace. Members of under-represented groups often experience isolation and frustration (Kanter, 1977; Tavris and Wade, 1984) in fields previously dominated by white men. Furthermore, the lack of role models—as with the absence of mentoring which we discussed earlier—often makes it difficult to hone the communicative strategies that lead to success in a given workplace. A lack of exposure to other employees impedes the kind of networking that is important for career advancement (Kanter, 1977; Morrison, White, and Van Velsor, 1992; Stewart, 1982). Additionally, minority members of an organization often feel pressured to have to outperform the majority members in order to prove themselves, to be accepted, and to alter preconceptions about the group they represent (Kanter, 1977; Lee, 1994; Morrison, White, and Van Velsor, 1992; Tavris and Wade, 1984).

In 1987, Cynthia Berryman-Fink and Virginia Eman-Wheeless predicted that as more women begin to fill the management slots, "the male-oriented management model is likely to give way to a flexible style that integrates traditional female behaviors and skills with traditional male behaviors" (p. 91). An integrative flexible style may be accepted in theory; however, whether the cause is bias, stereotyping, or lack of exposure, research during the past three decades clearly demonstrates that women in U.S. culture still experience barriers in the workplace. We believe that while the shift in qualities currently valued in professional settings reflects a transition, significant change will not be achieved until human "traits" (behaviors) and gender stereotypes are uncoupled.

SEXUAL HARASSMENT: COMMUNICATING DOMINATION

In the previous section we examined how stereotyping may covertly affect women's professional progress. Sexual harassment, in contrast, is a form of *overt* communicative behavior that directly influences the environment and impedes workers' performance. Blatant forms of workplace sexual harassment, such as the demand for a worker's sexual favors in response to threats or promises (termed *quid pro quo*), have been recognized as illegal since the passage of Title VII of the Civil Rights Act in 1964. Yet studies initiated in the mid-1970s uncovered the pervasiveness of sexual harassment in private industry, government agencies, and public companies and educational institutions (Bingham, 1996; Clair, McGoun, and Spirek, 1993; MacKinnon, 1979; Paetzold and O'Leary-Kelly, 1993; Steinhauer, 1997; Tong, 1984; Wood, 1993). In 1986 the Supreme Court expanded the definition of workplace sexual harassment to include a hostile work environment created by either direct or indirect offensive behavior. However, it was not until Anita Hill accused Supreme Court nominee

Clarence Thomas of sexual harassment in 1991 that the entire nation began to focus its attention on harassing conduct in the workplace.

As Cheris Kramarae (1992, p. 101) has established, "sexual harassment is not primarily about sex, or physical attraction, or about boys' and men's attempts to be 'nice' to girls or women. It is about the expression and enforcement of power and a binary gender hierarchy." Public awareness has led to the increased reporting of incidents of sexually harassing behavior: complaints filed with the Equal Employment Opportunity Commission rose from 3,300 suits filed in 1991 to 15,342 recorded cases in 1996 (Steinhauer, 1997; Swisher, 1994).[1]

Although victims of sexual harassment have the law on their side, there are several obstacles that may: (1) prevent some individuals from viewing their behavior as harassing and illegal; (2) influence how victims of harassment respond; and, (3) thwart initiatives to change the professional climate. We examine each of these challenges and conclude by suggesting ways to alter, and thereby diminish, instances of sexual harassment in the workplace.

Prior to the 1970s, the verbal and nonverbal messages that constitute what Tong has called the "little rapes," "looks," and "pats" to which women were subjected in the workplace were, of necessity, "largely accepted as an unpleasant fact of life" (1984, p. 65), since victims of harassment had no recourse. Part of the challenge of changing the cultural climate has been definitional: to rename behaviors that may have been tolerated in the past when victims had no other choice but are now recognized as illegal as well as abusive. Julia Wood (1993) suggests that sexual harassment is fundamentally a communication phenomenon: it rests on the interpretation of messages; "it is enacted through communication" (p. 10). Part of the challenge to increase public awareness of and to alter societal attitudes toward sexually harassing behavior is based on the terms we use, that is, the power of naming: "Naming sexual harassment in ways that call attention to its violence and wrongness is an achievement of critical importance. The emergence of harassment as a recognized phenomenon highlights the pivotal power of naming" (p. 15). The examples Wood offers reflect this power. Persons who were considered "objects of attention" may be regarded as "victims." Individuals whose unreciprocated behaviors

[1] These figures do not include both the vast number of cases that are settled before actual claims are filed as well as instances of sexual harassment that are never reported. Although sexual harassment affects both women and men, every study consistently indicates that women are overwhelmingly targets of sexual harassment.

were described as "pushy" or "forward" are now identified as "harass-ers." "Seduction," "advances," and "going too far" are now understood as "violations of individual rights" and in some instances "quid pro quos" (p. 15).

The above terms have legal as well as ethical ramifications inde-pendent of an individual sender's intent. However, the specific behaviors signified by these terms may be open to a range of interpre-tations. The "meanings" senders and receivers apply to a given behavior may vary according to the situation, the relationship, the workplace climate, and may be influenced as well by a range of other contextual factors.

In order to legally establish that sexual harassment has occurred, an individual plaintiff must prove that:

1. she or he, as a member of a protected class, has been an object of or has witnessed unwelcome behavior (for example, demands for sexual favors, inappropriate touching, lewd com-ments or gestures, insulting graffiti, etc.);
2. the behavior led to emotional, psychological, and/or physical conditions that affected the victim's ability to perform her or his duties; and
3. the employer knew or should have been aware of the harassing behavior and failed to intervene appropriately to halt and address the behavior.

Framing behaviors in legal terms is an important initial step in addressing sexual harassment. How one responds to a message or action that is unwelcome and that creates a "hostile climate" depends on a range of variables which include perceived power, perceived threat to one's future employment, the emotional and economic toll of con-fronting a harasser and identifying the behavior as harassment, and the extent to which a company policy on sexual harassment is defined and enforced. Robin Clair and her colleagues (1993) contend that these factors result in four general responses that move along a continuum of increasingly assertive behavior.

Characteristically, a victim's first two types of responses to unwel-come harassing behavior are avoidance and diffusion. Avoiding harassing behavior can take several forms: (a) trying to minimize con-tact with the harasser; (b) ignoring the harasser's behavior; (c) masking one's own response by doing nothing; (d) trying to negotiate a transfer to another unit within the organization to avoid contact; and, (e) leaving one's job (Clair, McGoun, and Spirek, 1993). In her study of gender conflicts, Borisoff (1992) found that the majority of undergraduate and graduate students she surveyed who experienced sexual harassment responded by quitting their jobs. The students rationalized their decisions by claiming that their jobs were temporary, that they did not believe it was worth their effort to register a complaint, or that they believed the company or boss would not take their complaint seriously. The majority of those students surveyed who reported having been harassed were women; however, several men indicated that they "thought" they had been harassed but were embarrassed to construe a sexual invitation as harassment because of societal attitudes toward male sexuality. This response supports Shereen Bingham's (1996) contention that "sexual scripts for masculinity encourage men to respond with confusion to sexual harassment, especially if the harasser is a physically attractive woman. Many authors claim that middle- and working-class, heterosexual, American culture expects men to be ready and eager to engage in sexual activity with women at all times" (p. 245).

Diffusion is a response whereby victims—women, in particular— may re-frame the harasser's behavior so as to avoid a direct confrontation and to maintain a working relationship with the individual (Clair, 1993; Clair, McGoun, and Spirek, 1993). Examples include dismissing or rationalizing the behavior by agreeing to interpret it as a joke or as unintentional (for example, "He didn't really mean anything by it," "That is just the way he is," "Men are just that way") or by accepting the behavior as part of the organizational culture (for example, "The other women don't seem to mind this type of behavior. Maybe I'm being too sensitive").

Although avoidance and diffusion responses may enable individuals to tolerate a climate or behavior which they intuitively know is inappropriate, unprofessional, and perhaps illegal, failing to stop this type of behavior and rationalizing its existence make them complicit in perpetuating a hostile climate in which they are victimized. Moreover, the emotional and psychic toll that tacit acceptance may exact over the course of one's professional lifetime has yet to be examined (Clair, McGoun, and Spirek, 1993). Prior to the enactment of legislation that identified certain behaviors as sexual harassment and, therefore, illegal, many women felt they had no option but to endure harassing behaviors if they wanted to keep their jobs. There was no recourse but to put up with the behavior or to seek another job. We concur with Wood's (1993) assertion that naming behavior provides legitimacy and clout to resistance. We would further suggest that individuals who, for whatever reason, have tried to tolerate such situations may experience an added level of ambivalence, anxiety, and guilt. They may know they are victims yet feel unable or unwilling to engage in the confrontation necessary to change the situation (Clair, McGoun, and Spirek, 1993).

Negotiation and confrontation are the third and fourth communicative responses to sexual harassment according to Clair, McGoun, and Spirek (1993) and reflect increased assertiveness. Individuals who perceive behavior as harassing and want to thwart such behavior may attempt to negotiate a change either directly or indirectly. Statements such as "I don't find your jokes about women particularly funny" or "I'm not interested in an emotional or sexual involvement with you" may stave off some of the harassing behavior. However, if the jokes or pressure persists, indirect threats may be invoked: "I don't think your 'jokes' fit the climate management is trying to create" or "I doubt that our personnel department would condone your pressuring me." If negotiation fails to halt the harasser's behavior, individuals who are subject to this treatment may escalate their reactions to direct confrontation.

Clair and her associates (1993) distinguish negotiating behavior from confronting behavior in two ways. First, "confrontation is 'telling' not 'asking'" for the harassing behavior to stop (p. 213). A comment such as, "I have repeatedly asked you to stop pressuring me about a relationship. Let me be clear: your failure to stop at once is sexual harassment," explicitly connects the offensive behavior with the expectation for immediate change. Second, confrontation is more apt to be utilized in workplace settings "where sexual harassment charges are legitimated through organizational policy" (p. 213), and so workers are empowered to confront their harassers.

But it is not only the victims of harassment whose responses to unwelcome behavior need examination. Individuals in positions of power—particularly men—bear responsibility for scrutinizing their own behavior to be certain that they are not inadvertently assuming and communicating a degree of intimacy that is neither shared nor desired by a co-worker or subordinate. Treating subordinates respectfully is impossible when individuals sexualize or objectify those over whom they have power or choose to disregard messages that indicate that their behavior, however well intentioned, is unwelcome. In order to protect employees, to comply with the law, and to avoid litigation, private and public institutions have responded by developing and disseminating their written policies and procedures for maintaining a harassment-free work environment. In addition, employee training sessions that heighten the awareness of, and sensitivity to, the kinds of behaviors that constitute a hostile work environment may be beneficial (Berryman-Fink, 1993; Booth-Butterfield, 1986; Galvin, 1993; Herndon, 1994). Such training often includes the use of outside consultants, training films, simulations, and case studies.

For training to be effective, however, it must do more than merely articulate the types of behaviors that have been legally identified as sexual harassment. Truly productive training would attempt to alter the perceptions, beliefs, and attitudes of all employees. Admittedly, this is hard to accomplish because, as we explained in chapter 1, stereotypes about gender—as well as stereotypes about culture, race, sexual orientation, religion—are often deep-seated and are difficult to dispel. However, exposing individuals to the existence and impact of abuses of power in a range of communicative dimensions and organizational climates and identifying their connection to myths and realities about gendered communication may shape new attitudes and influence behavioral change. Below we identify three areas organizations should address:

1. *Provide Appropriate Role Models.* Although there may be a wide range of acceptable communication styles that comprise any organizational culture (for example, formal and informal, competitive and collaborative, team orientation versus individual orientation), employees get their cues about what type of communication is allowable, acceptable, and appropriate from those at the highest levels of the organization. Thus, according to Sandra Herndon, "the responsibility for creating and supporting" any changes, and for setting the tone, "lies with upper management" (1994, p. 132).

Whether the organization is a large private corporation, a government agency, an academic institution, a law firm, or a small business, if those at the top tolerate or evidence sexually harassing behavior, or view such behavior as "harmless fun" or "benign flirtation," this will become the standard others in the organization may perceive as acceptable. However, if those in power communicate in ways that reflect respect for others, this, in turn, will define the professional climate.

2. *Acknowledge Inherent Power Imbalances.* Power (actual or perceived) is one essential variable contributing to sexual harassment. Three distinct types of power imbalances may make individuals especially vulnerable to the abuse and/or misuse of power. First, a perceived power imbalance may occur when one is a member of a margin-

alized group that is clearly dominated by members of another group. For example, sexual harassment by individuals who were at the same professional rank has been exacerbated when women entered workplace settings that have been traditionally the domain of men. Second, power imbalances exist within the internal hierarchical structure of institutions. Professors hold the power of the grade over students, bosses hold the power of salary and promotion over subordinates, and officers in the military hold the power of advancement over new recruits. Yet the mere fact of these power inequities does not account for why incidents of sexual harassment occur. Women are professors, and bosses, and captains; men may be in subordinate positions in relationship to women. Yet studies consistently confirm that women are the prime targets of sexual harassment. This suggests a third level of power imbalance—rooted in the relationship between male dominance and the gender socialization of women and men. Catherine MacKinnon claims that sexual harassment "eroticizes women's subordination" (1979, pp. 220–21). Sexual harassment, according to Tong, is "an extremely concrete way to remind women that their subordination as a gender is intimately tied to their sexuality, in particular to their reproductive capacities." (1984, p. 83).

3. *Examine Gender-Stereotyped Communication Styles.* In chapters 2 and 3, we explored verbal and nonverbal behaviors associated with gender. Berryman-Fink (1993) and Herndon (1994) suggest that effective training would encourage individuals to monitor their communication and to consider how verbal and nonverbal behavior may be (mis)construed. For example, if women engage in greater degrees of self-disclosure or in more smiling behavior in the workplace, whether as indications of friendliness and affiliation or because they have been socialized to "perform" expressiveness, men may interpret such acts as a sign of sexual interest (Berryman-Fink, 1993; Bingham, 1996; Borisoff and Hahn, 1993; Borisoff and Victor, 1998). Similarly, women and men may have experienced different degrees of control over personal space. As we have established in chapter 3, men who are accustomed to being afforded more space (than are women) as a result of their greater degrees of power may not be aware that approaching a woman too closely may be interpreted as an "intrusion," an "invasion," and/or as a "violation" of her personal space (Borisoff and Victor, 1998; Jones, 1994; Wood, 1994).

While we cannot assume that members of the workforce will become experts in all nuances of communication, we can raise their level of awareness about discrepancies between intention and interpretation and how communication behaviors may be a potent source of conflict. According to Berryman-Fink (1993, p. 276) "Since men and women are constrained by sex-role socialization, both sexes must work together to break free of conditioning, to overcome misunderstandings, to eliminate interactional power differences, and to create a workplace culture that is equitable, professional, and free of sexual harassment."

CHILD CARE: MAINTAINING DIFFERENCES IN RESPONSIBILITY

The next section of this chapter considers the impact of child care and other family needs on the careers of women and men. In 1993, the Family and Medical Leave Act was signed into law in the United States. This law requires any employer with more than fifty employees to grant up to twelve weeks of unpaid leave to a worker who needs to care for a new baby, an adopted child, an ill family member, or to recover from his or her own illness, after which the worker is entitled to return to the same or to an equivalent position. Although in spirit this law applies equally to men and to women, both societal gender expectations and attitudes about "dropping out of" the workplace to provide care for family members lead women and men to exercise this right unequally. In addition, the legal definition of "family" further limits those workers whose relationships are not officially sanctioned or recognized from exercising these basic rights.

As we have seen in the previous chapter, in the vast majority of heterosexual families, women retain primary responsibility for the home and for child rearing, in addition to their full-time jobs in the workplace (Blumstein and Schwartz, 1983; Hochschild, 1990; Holmes, 1996). Even when a woman chooses not to have children, these responsibilities can take the form of expectations that she function as caregiver to the other significant members of her extended family, such as her aging parents. Hence, women are often faced with pressure to integrate home and work responsibilities.

The media infrequently explore the conflicting demands facing working women with dependent children in a sympathetic fashion. Despite the fact that nearly 50 percent of married women earn half or more of their family's income and more than 30 percent of U.S. families are headed by one parent (Chira, 1992; Gabor, 1995), many contemporary women, influenced by popular mediated images of motherhood "are haunted by the ghost of the mythical 1950's television mother—one that most today cannot be, even if they wanted to" (Chira, 1992, p. A1). Because of a paucity of role models, guidelines for balancing caregiving and professional lives are unclear. According to Susan Chira (1992), women are caught between "a fictional ideal" and economic realities. "The old images," she contends, "linger, but they fit fewer people's lives" (p. A1).

A recent article in The *New York Times* suggests that women must accept and adapt to the traditional career paths for men in order to succeed professionally (Dobrzynski, 1996). According to gender and race relations consultant Robin Ely, "To be successful in a lot of companies, a woman has to conform to the image of someone who doesn't have an outside life, who doesn't have a family, and who doesn't have any interests outside of work" (cited in Dobrzynski, 1996, p. D19). Moreover, the same society "that gives women primary responsibility for children . . . does not furnish adequate child care" (Uchitelle, 1990, p. A1). The observations by Barbara Ehrenreich and Deidre English in 1989 were prescient. They summarized the frustration of professional women in the 1980s, a frustration that persists in the 1990s: "The 'fast track,' with its . . . toxic work load, remains the only track to success. As a result, success is indeed usually incompatible with motherhood— as well as with any engaged active form of fatherhood. . . . [I]t is the corporate culture itself that needs to slow down to a human pace" (p. 58).

The concern about child care is also echoed in academic works. In his work on women and men in management, Powell (1993) contends that when women endeavor to embrace and to follow paths of "success" that have been defined by men, while simultaneously accepting (and being expected to) shoulder the major responsibility for childrearing and homemaking, they are often forced to make uncomfortable choices. For many career women, their personal lives suffer: "Fewer female managers than male managers are married or have children. Looking at the ranks of top management, over 90% of male top executives are married and have children, whereas less than half of female top executives are married and have children" (p. 201).

Morrison and her colleagues (1992) found that one of the major factors to derail women on their career paths is the difficulty of integrating home life and work. This is especially hard for women, they argue, who must hide or downplay their personal lives so as to avoid negative scrutiny from colleagues and superiors: "They are scrutinized more closely than men, and they are judged on their personal life as well as on their job performance. If they indicate to more senior executives that their personal life is important, the suspicion that it will take precedence over their career grows. And on the basis of that suspicion, a woman's performance may be suspect or her advancement slowed" (pp. 113–14). Thus, what women communicate in the workplace may either explicitly or implicitly challenge or reinforce the stereotypes that coworkers, superiors, and subordinates have about women's commitment to their work or private life. For example, the need to prioritize their decisions and the challenge of trying to create a balance in their lives informed the responses of the seventy-six female executives Morrison and her colleagues (1992) interviewed: "With few exceptions . . . [those interviewed decided] to put their career first and squeeze in whatever else in life they can around it" (p. 114).

Juggling career and family responsibilities is difficult. Perhaps more disturbing, though, is that these concerns are devalued in our culture. Harlan and Weiss's (1982) study of one hundred managers revealed that women's and men's marital and parenting status are regarded unequally in our culture:

> For men, marriage and family have been seen as indications of stability and maturity, as well as a sign that traditional values and norms were being upheld. In addition, marriage has proved helpful to many managers' careers because of the roles taken on by their wives. Such roles include providing emotional support, aiding in time management, providing social contacts, and entertaining important organizational members and clients. For women managers, marital and parenting statuses have shown no clear-cut relationship to success. (p. 66)

Further, the absence of a support person to perform the "wifely" functions in the lives of women professionals may have a debilitating effect on their careers.

Hochschild's (1990) study of fifty heterosexual nuclear families where both parents work outside the home revealed that in many households there has been little change in the past two decades in terms of the amount of time husbands contribute to housework and child care. Out of necessity, many women have taken on this "second shift" while trying to negotiate for their partner's increased participation. According to a recent study by the Family and Work Institute, "women still do 87 percent of the shopping, 81 percent of the cooking, 78 percent of the cleaning and 63 percent of the bill-paying" (Holmes, 1996, p. 5). It is not surprising that the majority of men continue to resist engaging in tasks that have been the conventional domain of women—tasks, moreover, that are traditionally devalued because of that association with women's unpaid work.

In 1973, Young and Willmott predicted that by the twenty-first century, a more symmetrical heterosexual nuclear family will emerge; a family in which both partners will work outside the home and will work within the home. "[Then there will be] two demanding jobs for the wife and two for the husband. The symmetry will be complete" (p. 278). Sociologists Jean Stockard and Miriam Johnson (1980) and psychologist Sandra Bem (1993) caution that this symmetry cannot occur until attitudes toward caring for home and family are regarded more positively. Happily, many couples in the studies conducted by Kessler and McRae (1982), Blumstein and Schwartz (1983), Cohen (1987), and Hochschild (1990) make their home and their relationship a priority. These couples suffered the least amount of stress and reported the greatest relationship satisfaction. In this form of "collaborative couple," partners share in financial responsibilities, child care, decision making, and are mutually involved in each other's lives (Barnett and Rivers, 1996).

University of Washington professor Pepper Schwartz suggests "peer marriage" as another term to signify a balancing between responsibilities of work and child care (cited in Gabor, 1995). In peer marriages, "[the] husband and wife trade career priorities back and forth, accommodating each other's personal and professional needs as well as those of their families, depending on what stage of family and work life each is in" (Gabor, 1995, p. 98). This type of relationship also stresses the collaborative approach to addressing issues and responsibilities. These changes, according to Gabor (1995), "test the oldest, most fundamental emotional and practical assumptions about married life: along with reallocating household chores, they are redefining age-old gender roles and the balance of power within families" (p. 48).

Studies indicate that men, like women, express a range of attitudes toward family and work (Barnett and Rivers, 1996; Cohen, 1987; Gerson, 1993; Ross, 1994). In her study on men's commitment to work and family, sociologist Kathleen Gerson (1993) identified three distinct attitudes. First are traditional "breadwinners" who connect their identity with the man-as-provider role and view women as nurturers/caretakers, thereby perpetuating the essentialist division of roles explained in chapter 4. The second attitude expressed by what Gerson calls "autonomous" men, support women's rights to pursue careers; however, their "vision of economic and social equality does not extend to the domestic sphere. . . . [T]hey espouse the equal right to be free while resisting the equal responsibility for domestic work and child rearing" (Gerson, 1993, p. 267). The third category of men Gerson identifies consists of "involved fathers" who, "uncomfortable with male dominance in the home as well as the workplace . . ., have concluded that men and children as well as women benefit from more equal sharing" (p. 267).

It is important to remember, as we have established in chapter 4, that "fathering," like "mothering," is a societal construct, shaped by a given society, culture, and historical moment. "A man does not come to fatherhood in a vacuum. His paternal identity, expressed in fathering his children, is embedded in a life-historical, intrapsychic, and interpersonal context" (Ross, 1994, p. 48). For many people, work and family identities are currently in flux. The same forces that have led to traditional beliefs about how women should "mother" have informed the construction of fatherhood. Some of the challenges women have encountered in trying to extend their roles beyond the confines of societal expectations have also confronted those men who want to change expected behaviors. Each has moved in the opposite direction: many working women want to demonstrate that they are committed professionals while they are simultaneously expected to retain primary responsibility for their home and family; many working men want to become more active and involved in their family life while they are simultaneously expected to retain primary responsibility as wage earner.

Because male identity is so deeply anchored in work, the potential repercussions for being perceived as putting family life first may make men "even more nervous" about challenging cultural values and the expectations of others (Span, 1995, p. 56). The fear of long-term effects on their careers is real. Real, too, is the fear of how they will be viewed by a society that privileges the male domain and devalues those activities associated with women (Bem, 1993; Borisoff and Hahn, 1995b; Gerson, 1993; Ross, 1994). Despite the potential risks, studies indicate a shift in men's attitudes (if not in their actions) which challenge the stereotypes of masculinity while encouraging male bonding and supportiveness (Keen, 1991; Kimmel, 1987; Levant, 1996; Stoltenberg, 1990). Not only do "the majority of husbands now consider fathering more psychologically rewarding than their jobs" (Barnett and Rivers, 1996, p. 104), many men see paternity leave and other time spent with children as a valuable opportunity to bond with them (Span, 1995).

In 1993, 205,000 men between 25 and 59 were taking care of the home rather than earning a wage, a 49 percent increase since 1989, according to the Bureau of Labor Statistics (cited in Gabor, 1995, p. 46). Yet it remains to be seen to what degree this represents an active *choice* on the part of the men involved, rather than a result of other circumstances, such as diminished employment prospects, which may have led these men to leave the paid workforce. While a survey by Robert Half International reported that "nearly a third of the nation's largest companies offered paternity leave . . . only 1.3 percent of eligible men used it" (Span, 1995, p. 54). The fact that in many companies paternity leave is unpaid, coupled with how men felt they would be viewed for taking paternity leave, were cited as the major reasons that dissuaded new fathers from taking advantage of this benefit.

Not all companies, however, merely maintain family care policies on the books. Increasingly, many organizations recognize that women's and men's outlooks and obligations to meet the needs of their immediate and extended families have changed. Some employers have come to recognize that they must be responsive to these needs if they want to retain their best employees. For example, Aetna Life and Casualty and IBM found that they were losing many of their top performing women employees after they gave birth. These companies responded by extending the length of their child care leave policies in order to retain these workers (Aburdene and Naisbitt, 1992). Other companies including Gannett, MCI, and Corning have developed an impressive track record for increasing the numbers of women in top management positions. They have done so by implementing more aggressive mentoring programs, by adopting policies that enable women to balance job and family duties, and by not penalizing women who initially decline promotions because of caregiving responsibilities (Aburdene and Naisbitt, 1992; Castro, 1990).

Similarly, when men are compensated for taking paternity leave and are confident that their careers will not be threatened, their ability and willingness to assume familial obligations also increases: When Lotus changed its policy in the mid-1990s and offered one-month paid leaves to new fathers, nearly 40 percent of their male employees availed themselves of this opportunity (Span, 1995). These examples are indicative of the significant increase in the number of companies that are actively assisting employees with their family leave needs—an increase from 110 in 1978 to well over 7,000 in the early 1990s (Aburdene and Naisbitt, 1992). This assistance comes in many forms: providing alternative work patterns (job sharing, flextime, part-time work, etc.); parental leaves for either parent; child care support (on-site facilities, consortium daycare facilities, vouchers for day care costs, referral services, etc.). Such programs would enable working women and men to assume caretaking responsibilities for any family member who requires their help.

Despite these positive initiatives, the extent to which most companies actively encourage employees to utilize their child care and family care leave policies remains a matter of contention. The Family and Work Institute developed the Family Friendly Index to assess the extent to which companies provide these, as well as other health-care related policies, to employees. Although the index suggests that many companies are making a concerted effort to create policies that acknowledge the changing needs of its employees, *the vast majority* of companies, according to the Family and Work Institute copresident, Dana Friedman, have done little to alter the work environment in order to meet employees' needs (cited in Aburdene and Naisbitt, 1992). More aggressive and pervasive steps are required if we are to support women's and men's abilities to share fully and equally in balancing work and family. But this shift is not likely to occur until there is a fundamental recognition that the structure of the world of work still reflects the assumption of the traditional family and division of labor, an assumption that may be more indicative of tradition rather than of reality.

GENDER IN THE "VIRTUAL" OFFICE

Advances in technology augur new potentials for restructuring the workplace and for addressing the difficulties workers confront when they are required to balance their family needs with the need to be in an office setting. Daphne Spain (1992) has studied the relationships between gender, use of space, and occupational segregation. In her multicultural study, *Gendered Spaces*, Spain has established that women at the end of the twentieth century are more likely to be working in secretarial and clerical jobs than they were at the beginning of the century, when those occupations were not nearly as sex-segregated as they are presently (p. 201). Spain examined spatial segregation in the workplace and the impact of spatial control (or the lack of it) on the status and earning potential of female-dominant professions, such as clerical, teaching, and nursing, versus the "closed door" managerial, administrative, or executive occupations more likely to be held by men. Given empirical studies in which executives define privacy as "the ability to control information and space" and control others' access to one's workplace (p. 218), increasing numbers of workers whose dwellings are also their workplaces will undoubtedly have further implications for issues of gender and occupational segregation.

It is estimated that between six to eight million workers currently telecommute (Hildreth, 1996). Some benefits of "virtual offices"— where individuals perform their wage labor on computers located in their homes—are obvious: employers save on space costs; they are able to hire and retain qualified, motivated workers who reside a considerable distance from the office. According to Shaw (1996) telecommuters work an average of two additional hours per day and accomplish approximately 15 percent more work than their coworkers. From the employee's perspective, telecommuters may save on transportation and wardrobe costs (although how equipment, related insurance costs, and utilities costs are negotiated with employers may offset some of these savings); they may be able to attend to personal and family-related tasks that are difficult to accomplish when one is restricted to a conventional work schedule or confined to a workplace outside the home; options for deciding where to live increase when day-to-day commuting is no longer a requisite for employment (Ahrentzen, 1992; Ford and McLaughlin, 1995; McQuarrie, 1994; Snyder, 1996). Although redefining the workplace offers the above potential benefits, several concerns have resulted.

First, the majority of the behaviors associated with effective management (summarized earlier in this chapter) are predicated on face-to-face interaction. The absence of face-to-face communication has implications for the negotiation of performance expectations and supervision (Snyder, 1996). Second, lack of visibility at a common workplace affects the professional climate between and among workers, and it may also impede a worker's professional advancement (McQuarrie, 1994). According to Juliet Schor (1991), part of one's job performance and value within an organization is gauged by how effectively one networks both within and outside the office setting. Part of this attribution is related to how much "face time" employees put in at the office. We have yet to see how telecommuting will affect workers' networking, mentoring, and promotion opportunities. However, it is clear that isolation may significantly affect the telecommuter, and women who may have already experienced the negative effects of spatial limitations in conventional work environments may find themselves further isolated from opportunities to improve their work status if they choose to work at home. Some of the metaphors used to describe the workplace include "professional community," "home away from home," and "family" (Eldib and Minoli, 1995; Hochschild, 1997;

Kinsman, 1987). For telecommuters, the impact of the loss of these in-person connections to other workers which otherwise provide friendship, support, help, and even, on occasion, commiseration may be considerable.

Although working at home may appear at first to "solve" the issue of child care, this assumption is misleading. Performing wage work at home is no guarantee that an employee will be afforded privacy. In fact, requisite work conditions may be even more difficult to achieve. According to Mitch Betts (1995), many companies expect or require that employees who work from their homes make other formal child care arrangements. Technology will not eliminate the need for employees to dedicate attention to their work, while caregivers need to attend to those in their care. A final concern may be present for women who assume professional roles but enact them within a space traditionally associated with domestic functions. If women who perform wage work at home do not have the opportunity to display the external markers that signal a separation between domestic and professional spheres, others (and eventually the workers themselves) may come to expect that they are available, accessible, and responsible for domestic and family-related chores which encroach on their work (Ahrentzen, 1992). How workers negotiate these conflicting demands within the same space may give new meaning to Hochschild's "second shift" (1990) and may threaten to imprison women within the rooms they now own.

Virginia Woolf ended her essay, "A Room of Her Own," by pondering the effects that gendered experiences of poverty and privilege have on the mind:

> [A]nd I thought how unpleasant it is to be locked out; and I thought how it is worse perhaps to be locked in; and, thinking of the prosperity of the one sex and of the poverty and insecurity of the other and of the effect of tradition upon the mind of a writer. (1929, p. 188)

As women and men continue to negotiate the issues that impinge upon their professional and personal identities, perhaps we can begin to think not of being locked out or of being locked in, but rather of opening doors.

Suggested Activities

A. Focus on "Professional" Attitudes in the Workplace

Either individually or as part of a group project, interview professionals who are responsible for making hiring decisions in the field(s) you wish to enter. Some suggested interview questions include:

a. What personal qualities do you look for in an applicant?

b. How do you determine whether an applicant possesses these qualities?

c. What communication skills are required for this position?

d. What professional attire is appropriate for this position?

Discuss with other members of the class the extent to which these responses support or challenge the existence of a gender-neutral workplace.

B. Focus on Influencing Professional Identity

Identify specific individuals who contributed to your personal occupational aspirations. Discuss the presence or absence of gender stereotypes in those individuals' perceptions of given professions and the reactions of family and friends to others' occupational choices.

C. Focus on Appropriate and Inappropriate Workplace Behavior

Working in pairs or groups, generate a list of behaviors which would be considered "acceptable" in social contexts and a list of those that could be construed as sexual harassment. What factors influence each interpretation? How do power and gender variables enter into these determinations?

D. Focus on Professional Appearance

Bring a magazine portrayal of a "professional" woman and a "professional" man to class. Using the section in this chapter on appearance and hiring decisions, discuss whether or not the magazine images signify competence and professionalism. How are these images related to stereotypes about gender? socio-economic class? ethnicity?

Chapter Six

Changing the
Gendered Scripts

[the worst part of] living in a prison without bars is that you aren't even aware of the screens that shut out the horizon.

— Simone de Beauvoir, *Memoirs of a Dutiful Daughter*

For de Beauvoir's protagonist, a "prison without bars" is a metaphor for society during the mid-twentieth century—a society which, through its unwritten rules and expectations for women's lives, restricts their quest for autonomy. Although there have been decided changes since de Beauvoir published her memoir, many barriers to effective egalitarian communication between men and women still exist. Today, many people recognize the metaphoric "bars" that constrain them and they are endeavoring to remove the "screens" that block the path to equality.

EFFECTING CHANGE:
EXPANDING HUMAN POTENTIAL

As we have seen throughout this text, gender-based stereotypes are manifested through communicative acts. All behavior, whether or not it is intentional, has potential "message value" and exists within a social context. For example, the choice to be silent tells spectators as much about a person as the choice to speak.

Although there is no aspect of the communication discipline in which gender is not a factor, comparatively few texts deal with the associations between the performance of gender in verbal and nonverbal communication and the relative power associated with "masculinity" or "femininity." Texts in our discipline tend either to address gender only tangentially or else to offer essentialized pronouncements about the communicative behavior of women and men.

College and universities prepare students to enter occupations that continue to be shaped by unarticulated gender stereotypes. For the prospective therapist, counselor, or mediator, a study of dyadic communication and interview techniques is incomplete unless one is cognizant of the potential impact of gendered communication styles and power inequities on the interview. Similarly, the businessperson who studies group dynamics needs to be apprised of the possible effects of differing sex-role expectations in the workplace. The hierarchies of small groups, leadership, and role-taking functions are affected by differences in behavior and the belief systems which support them. Future public speakers in law, politics, education, or any other field need to be aware of how their enaction of gender stereotypes may facilitate or impede their listeners' reception of their message. All of us, in the most intimate of the interpersonal relationships of our lives, will be able to share openly and honestly with each other only if we are sensitive to the potential power imbalances between us that may be exacerbated by gender-linked communication differences.

In this book, we have introduced you to the connection between gender stereotypes and power inequities and discussed their impact in personal and professional settings. While it would be impossible to address adequately every possible aspect of communication in a book of this scope, we have tried to present you with representative examples of contexts in which assumptions about gender affect communication. We have maintained throughout that although traditional "masculine" modes of behavior have been generally considered normative, stronger, and more desirable than communicative acts that signify "femininity," neither "masculine" nor "feminine" communicative acts are inherently better or worse, stronger or weaker. Rather, it is the interpretation placed upon these respective styles that has led people to value one over the other—to reward certain behaviors and punish others. It is that interpretation that we call into question.

We also have questioned empirical studies and anecdotal observations which assume that reported sex differences in behavior are applicable to all men or to all women. Often such studies ignore similarities between these groups, exaggerate differences, and do not consider other factors (for example, power, context, the nature of the interaction setting, etc.) that may influence findings (Aries, 1987; Cirksena and Cuklanz, 1992; Henley and Kramarae, 1994; Wood, 1992). Often these studies are conducted using white, heterosexual, middle-class subjects whose experiences and perspectives do not speak to the experiences of homosexuals and members of other races, cultures (or subcultures), and social classes (Thorne, 1986).

Instead of perpetuating a biologically deterministic view which assumes women's and men's "essential" differences, we have looked to other contemporary models, such as the notion that gender is a series of "acts" learned and performed (Butler, 1990; Goffman, 1979) to account for the range of behaviors displayed by women and by men in a given context. According to Julia Wood (1994), standpoint theory may also be a productive way to examine gender and communication. *Standpoint theory* focuses on individuals' positions within social hierarchies (such as gender, race, and class) and examines how power relationships inform people's perspectives. Wood contends that, "the particular standpoint that an individual has in a society guides what she or he knows, feels, and does, and directs an individual's understanding of social life as a whole" (1994, p. 51). Standpoint theory requires a consideration of the multiple and interconnected conditions and experiences of gender, race, and class as socially structured relations, influencing all aspects of the communication process.

However, as we have seen in the previous chapters, in addition to recognizing the socially constructed perspectives from which women and men perceive their world, there is still a pressing need to overcome the barrier of male dominance in the workplace and in the home. We need to address the concerns and self-perceptions of those whose subordinate status is the result of others' dominance. For a long time women have recognized and have challenged the effects of these attitudes on their lives. Increasingly, men are questioning the effects of these prescriptions on their own lives as well. Although traditional masculine styles of stoicism, aggressiveness, and inexpressiveness have had "considerable utility in maintaining men's power" (Cameron, 1992, p. 77), some men are beginning to reassess their communicative styles and broaden their repertoire to express a wider range of emotions, such as hurt, disappointment, fear, and shame. Along with reconceptionalizing their behaviors, these men are redefining traditional masculine roles. In chapter 5 we indicated the importance of men's growing valuation of parenthood and their desire to become actively involved in nurturing children as an example of this redefinition.

Changing the gendered scripts, however, requires a simultaneous scrutiny of what might be lost in the process. Redressing inequities necessitates that some people give up their relative privilege. As one theorist asks rhetorically, "If men no longer share a distinctive identity based on their economic role as family providers, then what is a man? If men can no longer claim special rights and privileges based on their unique responsibilities and contributions, then how can they justify their power? If men can no longer assert patriarchal control by being the heads of their households, then what kind of relationships will they establish with women and children?" (Gerson, 1993, pp. 259–60).

How we answer these questions will affect the lives of men, women, and the children of the future. Will the "legitimacy" afforded traditional male power, privilege, and communicative behaviors be replaced by other markers of power and privilege? Will reconceptualizing and revaluing roles and behaviors remove the stigma of the separate poles we now define as masculine and feminine, and enable us instead to regard "the biology of sex . . . (as a) 'minimal presence' in human social life"? (Bem, 1993, p. 192).

Instead of perpetuating the notion of gendered styles as biologically determined polar opposites, we have suggested ways that women and men might effectively use the strategies conventionally associated with the other sex. In order for these strategies to be adopted, we must remove deprecatory associations for "feminine" behavior. As we have noted, the stereotypically "feminine" styles of communication have been considered weaker, less direct, and less assertive than "masculine" styles in that they seek affirmation and approval of other communicators. However, if we reconceptualize these categories—identifying them instrumentally as "invitational" or "dominating" rather than as feminine or masculine, we are better able to reinterpret behavior. This may move us closer to removing the androcentric bias which prescribes, limits, and values men's and women's roles and behaviors differentially.

We realize that men's and women's communication will not be valued equally until the social institutions that anoint one mode over another are changed. We can begin that journey by looking at, by listening to, and by questioning the conventions that have been embraced by both traditional sex and gender stereotypes for so long. In the process, we can remove the remaining barriers that keep us "prisoners" in the gendered lives we have constructed. Only then will be able to reach out and understand each other.

References

Aburdene, P., and Naisbitt, J. (1992). *Megatrends for Women*. New York: Villard Books.

Adler, N. (April, 1994). Women managers in a global economy. *Training and Development*, 31–36.

Ahrentzen, S. B. (1992). Home as a workplace in the lives of women. In I. Altman and S. M. Low (Eds.), *Place Attachment*. New York: Plenum Press.

Allen, E. (February, 1993). Best news ever for working women. *Glamour*, 198–201; 225.

Argyle, M., Lalljee, M., and Cook, M. (1968). The effects of visibility on interaction on a dyad. *Human Relations* 21:3–17.

Aries, E. (1976). Interaction patterns and themes of male, female and mixed groups. *Small Group Behavior*, 7:7–18.

_____. (1982). Verbal and nonverbal behavior in single-sex and mixed-sex groups: Are traditional sex roles changing? *Psychological Reports*, 51: 127–34.

_____. (1987). Gender and communication. In P. Shaver and C. Hendrick (Eds.), *Sex and Gender*, 149–76. Newbury Park, CA: Sage Publications.

Arliss, L. (1991). *Gender Communication*. Englewood Cliffs, NJ: Prentice-Hall.

Austin, W. (1965). Some social aspects of paralanguage. *Canadian Journal of Linguistics*, 11:31–9.

Barnett, R., and Rivers, C. (June, 1996). Good news for families. *Ladies' Home Journal*, 102; 104; 106.

Bass, B. M., Krusell, J., and Alexander, R. A. (1971). Male managers' attitudes toward working women. *American Behavioral Scientist*, 15:221–36.

Baxter, L. A., and Montgomery, B. M. (1996). *Relating: Dialogue and Dialectics*. New York: Guilford Press.

Beck, A. (1988). *Love is Never Enough*. New York: Harper & Row.

Bederman, G. (1995). *Manliness and Civilization: A Cultural History of Gender and Race in the United States, 1880–1917*. Chicago: University of Chicago Press.

Bem, S. L. (1993). *The Lenses of Gender: Transforming the Debate on Sexual Inequality.* New Haven: Yale University Press.

Berkin, C. R., and Norton, M. B. (Eds.). (1979). *Women of America: A History.* Boston: Houghton Mifflin Co.

Berman, P. (1986). Young children's responses to babies: Do they foreshadow differences between maternal and paternal styles? In A. Fogel and G. F. Melson (Eds.), *Origins of Nurturance: Developmental, Biological, and Cultural Perspectives on Caregiving.* Hillsdale, NJ: Lawrence Erlbaum Associates.

Bernard, J. (1981). *The Female World.* New York: The Free Press.

Berryman-Fink, C. (1993). Preventing sexual harassment through male-female communication training. In G. L. Kreps (Eds.), *Sexual Harassment: Communication Implications.* Cresskill, NJ: Hampton Press, 267–80.

Berryman-Fink, C., and Eman-Wheeless, V. (1987). Male and female perceptions of women as managers. In L. P. Stewart and S. Ting-Toomey (Eds.), *Communication, Gender, and Sex Roles in Diverse Interaction Contexts*, 85–90. Norwood, NJ: Ablex.

Betts, M. (August 7, 1995). Telecommuting: the dark side. *Computerworld*, 55.

Bingham, S. G. (1996). Sexual harassment: On the job, on the campus. In J. T. Wood (Ed.), *Gendered Relationships*, 233–52. Mountain View, CA: Mayfield Publishing Co.

Blumen, J. L. (1994). The existential bases of power relationships: The gender role case. In H. L. Radtke and H. J. Stam (Eds.), *Power/Gender: Social Relations in Theory and Practice*, 108–35. Thousand Oaks, CA: Sage Publications.

Blumer, H. (1969). The nature of symbolic interactionism. In *Symbolic Interactionism: Perspective and Methods*, 2–21. Englewood Cliffs, NJ: Prentice-Hall.

Blumstein, P., and Schwartz, P. (1983). *American Couples: Money, Work, Sex.* New York: William Morrow & Co.

Bochner, S. (1982). The social psychology of cross-cultural relations. In S. Bochner (Ed.), *Cultures in Contact*, 5–44. New York: Pergammon Press.

Bohn, E., and Stutman, R. (1983). Sex-role differences in the relational control dimensions of dyadic interaction. *Women's Studies in Communication*, 6:96–104.

Booth-Butterfield, M. (Fall 1986). Recognizing and communicating in harassment-prone organizational climates. *Women's Studies in Communication*, 9:42–51.

Borisoff, D. (1992). Patterns of gender conflict: A closer look. *New Dimensions in Communication.* Proceedings of the New York State Speech Communication Association, VI:11–25.

_____. (1993). The effect of gender on establishing and maintaining intimate relationships. In L. P. Arliss and D. Borisoff (Eds.), *Women and Men*

Communicating: Challenges and Changes, 14–28. Fort Worth, TX: Holt, Rinehart, and Winston.

Borisoff, D., and Hahn, D. F. (Summer, 1993). Thinking with the body: Sexual metaphors. *Communication Quarterly*, 41(3): 253–60.

_____. (Fall, 1995a). From research to pedagogy: Teaching gender and communication. *Communication Quarterly*, 43:4, 381–93.

_____. (1995b). Gender power in context: A re-evaluation of communication in professional relationships. *New Dimensions in Communication*. Proceedings of the New York State Speech Communication Association, VIII:11–23.

_____. (1997a). The mirror in the window: Displaying our gender biases. In S. J. Drucker and G. Gumpert (Eds.), *Voices in the Street: Explorations in Gender, Media, and Public Space*, 101–17. Cresskill, NJ: Hampton Press.

_____. (1997b). Listening and gender: Values revalued. In M. Purdy and D. Borisoff (Eds.), *Listening in Everyday Life: A Personal and professional Approach*. 2d ed., 47–69. Lanham, MD: University Press of America.

Borisoff, D., and Merrill, L. (1991). Gender issues and listening. In D. Borisoff and M. Purdy (Eds.), *Listening in Everyday Life: A Personal and Professional Approach*, 59–85. Lanham, MD: University Press of America.

Borisoff, D., and Victor, D. A. (1998). *Conflict Management: A Communication Skills Approach*, 2d ed. Boston, MA: Allyn & Bacon.

Bradley, P. H. (March 1981). The folk-linguistics of women's speech: an empiral examination. *Communication Monographs*, 48:90.

Bredin, A. (December 23, 1995). Today's manager. *The West Side Spirit*, 6–9.

Brend, R. (1975). Male-female intonation patterns in American English. In B. Thorne and N. M. Henley (Eds.), *Language and Sex: Difference and Dominance*, 84–104. Rowley, MA: Newbury House.

Brown, P., and Levinson, S. (1978). Universals in language usage: politeness phenomena. In E. N. Goody (Ed.), *Questions and Politeness: Strategies in Social Interaction*, 256–89. Cambridge, England: Cambridge University Press.

Buck, R. (1977). Nonverbal communication of affect in preschool children: Relationships with personality and skin conductance. *Journal of Personality and Social Psychology*, 35:225–36.

_____. (1979). Individual differences in nonverbal sending accuracy and electrothermal responding: The externalizing-internalizing dimension. In R. Rosenthal (Ed.), *Skill in Nonverbal Communication: Individual Differences*. Cambridge, MA: Oelgeschlager, Gunn & Hain.

Butler, J. (1990). *Gender Trouble: Feminism and the Subversion of Identity*. New York: Routledge.

Cameron, D. (1992). *Feminism in Linguistic Theory*. London: MacMillan.

Cameron, D., McAlinden, F., and O'Leary, K. (1989). "Lakoff in Context: the Social and Linguistic Functions of Tag Questions." In J. Coates, and D.

Cameron (Eds.), *Women in Their Speech Communities: New Perspectives on Language and Sex*. London: Longman.

Canary, D. J., and Hause, K. S. (Spring, 1993). Is there any reason to research sex differences in communication? *Communication Quarterly*, 41(2): 129–44.

Carli, L. L. (1990). Gender, language and influence. *Journal of Personality and Social Psychology*, 56:565–76.

Castro, J. (Fall, 1990). Get set: Here they come. *Time and Women: The Road Ahead*, 50–52.

Chira, S. (October 4, 1992). New realities fight old images of mother. *New York Times*, A1; 32.

Cirksana, K., and Cuklanz, L. (1992). Male is to female as ____ is to ____: A guided tour of five feminist frameworks for communication studies." In L. Rakow (Ed.), *Women Making Meaning: New Feminist Directions in Communication*, 18–43. New York: Routledge.

Clair, R. P. (June, 1993). The use of framing devices to sequester narratives: Hegemony and harassment. *Communication Monographs*, 60(2): 113–36.

Clair, R. P., McGoun, M. J., and Spirek, M. M. (1993). Sexual harassment responses of working women: An assessment of current communication-oriented typologies and perceived effectiveness of the response. In G. L. Kreps (Ed.), *Sexual Harassment: Communication Implications*, 209–33. Cresskill, NJ: Hampton Press.

Coates, J. (1986). *Women, Men, and Language: Studies in Language and Linguistics*. London: Longman.

Cohen, T. (1987). Remaking men: Men's experiences becoming and being husbands and fathers and their implications for reconceptualizing men's lives. *Journal of Family Issues*, 8 (1): 57–77.

Collingwood, H. (November, 1995). Women as managers: Not just different—better. *Working Woman*, 14.

Collis, B., and Ollila, L. (1990). The effect of Computer use on grade 1 children's gender stereotypes about reading, writing, and computer use. *Journal of Research and Development in Education*, 24:14–20.

Cooper, P. (1993). Communication and gender in the classroom. In L. P. Arliss and D. Borisoff (Eds.), *Women and Men Communicating: Challenges and Changes*, 122–41. Fort Worth, TX: Holt, Rinehart, and Winston.

Courtright, J. A., Millar, F. E., and Rogers-Millar, L. E. (1979). Domineeringness and dominance: Replication and expansion. *Communication Monographs*, 46:179–92.

Cox, T., and Blake, S. (August, 1991). Managing cultural diversity: Implications for organizational competitiveness. *Academy of Management Executive*, 5(3): 45–46.

Crosby, F., and Nyquist, J. (1977). The female register: An empirical study of the Lakoff's hypotheses. *Language in Society*, 6:313–22.

Curt, C., and Nine, J. (1983). Hispanic-Anglo conflicts in nonverbal communication. In I. Albino (Ed.), *Perspectives Pedagogicas*. San Juan: Universidad de Puerto Rico.

Dass, K. (1986). Effect of gender identity on conversation. *Social Psychology Quarterly*, 49(4): 294–301.

Davis, F. B. (1992). *Fashion, Culture and Identity*. Chicago: University of Chicago Press.

Deaux, K., and Major, B. (1987), Putting gender into context: An interactive model of gender-related behavior. *Psychology Bulletin*, 94:369–89.

de Beauvior, S. (1952). *The Second Sex*. H. M. Parshley (Trans. and Ed.). New York: Bantam Books, Alfred A. Knopf.

_____. (1959). *Memoirs of a Dutiful Daughter*. H. Kirkup (Trans.). New York: Harper & Row.

DeWine, S. (August 1987). Female leadership in male dominated organizations. *ACA Bulletin*, 61:19–29

Dill, B. T. (1996). The dialectics of black womanhood. In J. W. Scott (Ed.), *Feminism and History*. New York: Oxford University Press.

Dindia, K. (1987). The effects of sex of subject and sex of partner on interruptions. *Human Communication Research* 3:345–71.

Dindia, K., and Allen, M. (1992). Sex differences in self-disclosure: A meta-analysis. *Psychological Bulletin*, 112(1): 106–24.

Dobrzynski, J. H. (November 6, 1996). Somber news for women on corporate ladder. *New York Times*, D1; D9.

Dolphin, C. Z. (1988). Beyond Hall: Variables in the use of personal space. *Howard Journal of Communications*, 1:23–38.

Duberman, L. (1975). *Gender and Sex in Society*. New York: Praeger Publishers.

Dubois, B. L., and Crouch, I. (1975). The question of tag questions in women's speech: They don't really use more of them, do they? *Language in Society*, 4:289–94.

Dubois, E. C., (Ed.). (1981). *Elizabeth Cady Stanton/Susan B. Anthony: Correspondence, Writings, Speeches*. New York: Schocken Books.

Duck, S. (1988). *Relating to Others*. Chicago: Dorsey.

_____. (1991). *Understanding Relationships*. New York: Guilford Press.

Duncan, S., and Fiske, D. W. (1977). *Face-to-Face Interaction*. Hillsdale, NJ: Erlbaum.

Eagly, A. H., Ashmore, R. D., Makhijani, M. G., and Longo, L. C. (1991). What is beautiful is good, but . . .: A meta-analytic view of research on the physical attractiveness stereotype. *Psychological Bulletin*, 110(2): 109–28.

Eagly, A. H., and Johnson, B. J. (1990). Gender and leadership style: A meta-analysis. *Psychological Bulletin*, 108:233–56.

Eagly, A. H., and Karau, S. J. (1991). Gender and the emergence of leaders: A meta-analysis. *Psychological Bulletin*, 60:685–710.

Eakins, B. W., and Eakins, R. G. (1978). *Sex Differences in Human Communication.* Boston: Houghton Mifflin Co.

Eccles, J., and Jacobs, J. (1986). Social forces shape math attitudes and performance. *Signs,* 11:367–80.

Edgar, T. (1994). Self-disclosure behaviors of the stigmatized: strategies and outcomes for the revelation of sexual orientation. In J. R. Ringer (Ed.), *Queer Words, Queer Images: Communication and the Construction of Homosexuality.* New York: New York University Press.

Edelsky, C. (1979). Question intonation and sex roles. *Language and Society,* 8:15–32.

Ehrenreich, B., and English, D. (July/August 1989). Blowing the whistle on the mommy track. *Ms.,* 56–58.

Eisler, R. (1987). *The Chalice and the Blade: Our History, Our Future.* San Francisco: Harper & Row.

Eldib, O. E., and Minoli, D. (1995). *Telecommuting.* Boston: Artech House.

Ellsworth, P. C., Carlsmith, J. M., and Henson, A. (1972). The stare as a stimulus to flight in human subjects: A series of field experiments. *Journal of Personality and Social Psychology,* 21:302–11.

Ellyson, S. L., Dovidio, J. F., Corson, R. L., and Vinicur, D. L. (1980). Visual dominance behavior in female dyads: Situational and personality factors. *Social Psychology Quarterly,* 42:328–36.

Epstein, C. F. (1981). *Women in Law.* New York: Basic Books.

_____. (January-February, 1991). Ways men and women lead. *Harvard Business Review,* 150–51.

Fagot, B. I. (1978). The influence of sex of child on parental reaction. *Developmental Psychology,* 10:554–50.

Fagot, B. I., Hagen, R., Leinbach, M. D., and Kronsberg, S. (1985). Differential reactions to assertive and communicative acts of toddler boys and girls. *Child Development,* 56:1499–1505.

Faludi, S. (1991). *Backlash: The Undeclared War Against American Women.* New York: Doubleday.

Fennema, E., and Sherman, J. (Winter 1977). Sex-related differences in mathematics achievement. *American Educational Research,* 14(1): 51–71.

Fish, M., Gross, A., and Sanders, J. (1986). The effect of equity strategies on girls' computer usage in school. *Computers in Human Behavior,* 2(2): 127–44.

Fishman, P. M. (1980). Conversational insecurity. In H. Giles, W. P. Robinson, and P. M. Smith (Eds.), *Language: Social Psychological Perspectives,* 127–32. New York: Pergammon Press.

_____. (1983). Interaction: The work women do. In B. Thorne, C. Kramarae, and N. Henley (Eds.), *Language, Gender and Society.* Rowley: MA Newbury House.

Fiske, E. P. (April 11, 1990). How to learn in colleges: Group study, many tests. *New York Times*, A1.

Flexner, E. (1968). *Century of Struggle: The Woman's Rights Movement in the United States*. New York: Atheneum.

Ford, R. C., and McLaughlin, F. (May–June, 1995). Questions and answers about telecommuting programs. *Business Horizons*, 66–72.

Forsythe, S. M. (1990). Effect of applicant's clothing on interviewer's decision to hire. *Journal of Applied Social Psychology*, 20:1579–95.

Forsythe, S., Drake, M. F., and Cox, C. E. (1985). Influence of applicant's dress on interviewer's selection decisions. *Journal of Applied Psychology*, 70:374–78.

Freedman, R. (1986). *Beauty Bound*. Lexington, MA: D. C. Heath.

Gabor, A. (November, 1995). Married with househusband. *Working Woman*, 46, 48, 50, 90, 99.

Gal, S. (1994). Between speech and silence: The problematics of research on language and gender. In C. Roman, S. Juhasz, and C. Miller (Eds.), *The Women and Language Debate: A Sourcebook*. New Brunswick, NJ: Rutgers University Press.

Galvin, J. M. (1993). Preventing the problems: Preparing faculty members for the issues of sexual harassment. In G. L. Kreps (Ed.), *Sexual Harassment: Communication Implications*, 257–66. Cresskill, NJ: Hampton Press.

Gaines, S. (1995). Relationships between members of cultural minorities. In J. T. Wood and S. W. Duck (Eds.), *Understanding Relationship Processes, 6: Off the Beaten Track: Understudied Relationships*, 51–88. Thousand Oaks, CA: Sage.

Garber, M. (1992). *Vested Interests: Cross-Dressing and Cultural Anxiety*. New York: HarperCollins.

Gerson, K. (1993). *No Man's Land: Men's Changing Commitments to Family and Work*. New York: Basic Books.

Gilligan, C. (1982). *In a Different Voice: Psychological Theory and Women's Development*. Cambridge: Harvard University Press.

Gilman, C. P. (1911/1971). *The Man-Made World; or our Androcentric Culture*. New York: Johnson Reprint. Cited in S. L. Bem (1993) *The Lenses of Gender: Transforming the Debate on Sexual Inequality*. New Haven: Yale University Press, p. 41.

Gleason, J. B. (1987). Sex differences in parent-child interaction. In C. Roman, S. Juhasz, and C. Miller (Eds.), *The Woman and Language Debate: A Sourcebook*. New Brunswick, NJ: Rutgers University Press.

Gleason, J. B., and Greif, E. B. (1983). Men's speech to young children. In C. Kramerae and N. Henley (Eds.), *Language, Gender and Society*. Rowley, MA: Newbury House.

Goffman, E. (1979). *Gender Advertisements*. New York: Harper & Row.

_____. (1977). The arrangement between the sexes. *Theory and Society*, 4:301–31.

Goleman, D. (April 10, 1990). Stereotypes of the sexes persisting in therapy. *New York Times*, C1; C10.

Graebner, A. (1982). Growing up female, In L. A. Samovar and R. E. Porter (Eds.), *Intercultural Communication: A Reader*. Belmont, CA: Wadsworth Publishing Co.

Graves, L., and Powell, G. N. (1988). An investigation of sex discrimination in recruiters' evaluations of actual applicants. Cited in G. N. Powell (1993), *Women and Men in Management*, 2d ed. Newbury Park, CA: Sage Publications.

Greif, E. B. (1980). Sex differences in parent-child conversations. In C. Kramarae (Ed.), *The Voices and Words of Women and Men*, 253–58. New York: Pergammon Press.

Grob, L. M., and Allen, M. (April, 1996). Sex differences in powerful/powerless language: A meta-analytic review. Paper presented to the Central States Communication Association, Minneapolis.

Grosz, E. (1994). *Volatile Bodies: Toward a Corporeal Feminism*. Bloomington: Indiana University Press.

Halberstadt, A., and Saitta, M. (1987). Gender, nonverbal behavior and perceived dominance: A test of the theory." *Journal of Personality and Social Psychology*, 53:257–72.

Hall, E. T. (1981). *The Silent Language*. New York: Anchor Doubleday.

Hall, J. (1984). *Nonverbal Sex Differences: Communication Accuracy and Expressive Style*. Baltimore: Johns Hopkins University Press.

Harlan, A., and Weiss, C. L. (1982). Sex differences in factors affecting managerial career advancement. In P. A. Wallace (Ed.), *Women in the Workplace*, 59–100. Boston, MA: Auburn House.

Harper, L. V., and Sanders, K. M. (1975). Preschool children's use of space: Sex differences in outdoor play. *Developmental Psychology*, 11:119.

Hartford, B. S. (1976). Phonological differences in the English of adolescent Chicanas and Chicanos. In B. L. Dubois and I. Crouch (Eds.), *The Sociology of the Languages of American Women*, 73–80. San Antonio, TX: Trinity University.

Haste, H. (1994). *The Sexual Metaphor: Men, Women, and the Thinking that Makes the Difference*. Cambridge: Harvard University Press.

Hatfield, E., and Rapson, R. (1993). *Love, Sex, and Intimacy: Their Psychology, Biology, and History*. New York: HarperCollins.

Heilman, M. E. (1984). Information as a deterrent against sex discrimination: The effects of applicant sex and information type on preliminary employment decisions. *Organizational Behavior and Human Performance*, 33:174–86.

Henley, N. M. (1973). Status and sex: Some touching observations. *Bulletin of the Psychonomic Society*, 2:91–93.

_____. (1977). *Body Politics: Power, Sex, and Nonverbal Communication*. Englewood Cliffs, NJ: Prentice-Hall.

Henley, N. M., and Kramarae, C. (1994). Gender, power, and miscommunication. In C. Roman, S. Juhasz, and C. Miller (Eds.), *The Women of Language Debate: A Sourcebook*, 382–406. New Brunswick, NJ: Rutgers University Press.

Henrique, D. (August 27, 1989). To American women: Sayonara. *New York Times*, A32.

Herndon, S. (1994). Gender and communication. In R. L. Ray (Ed.), *Bridging Both Worlds: The Communication Consultant in Corporate America*, 125–36. Lanham, MD: University Press of America.

Hildreth, S. (April 8, 1996). Trimming telecommuting's price tag. *Computerworld*, 100.

Hirschman, L. (December, 1973). Female-male differences in conversational interaction. Paper given at the meeting of the Linguistic Society of America, San Diego, California.

Hite, Shere. (1987). *Women and Love: A Cultural Revolution in Progress*. New York: Alfred A. Knopf.

Hochschild, A. (December, 1983). Smile wars: Counting the casualties of emotional labor. *Mother Jones*, 35–42.

_____. (1990). *The Second Shift*. New York: Avon Books.

Hochschild, A. H. (April 20, 1997). There's no place like work. *New York Times Sunday Magazine*, 51–55; 81; 84.

Holmes, J. (1984). Hedging your bets and sitting on the fence. *Te Reo*, 27:47–62.

Holmes, S. A. (December 15, 1996). Sitting pretty: Is this what women want. *New York Times Week in Review*, sec. 4:1; 5.

hooks, b. (1984). *Feminist Theory: From Margin to Center*. Boston: South End Press.

Hoyles, C. A. (1988). *Girls and Computers: General Issues and Case Studies of Logo in the Mathematics Classroom*. London: University of London Press.

Hughes, K. A. (September 1, 1987). Businesswomen's broader latitude in dress codes goes just so far: Male executives also suffer for their sartorial mistakes. *Wall Street Journal*, 33.

Hyde, J. S., Fennema, E., and Lamon, S. J. (1990). Gender differences in mathematics performance: A meta-analysis. *Psychological Bulletin*, 107:139–45.

Hyde, J. S., and Linn, M. C. (1988). Gender differences in verbal ability: A meta-analysis. *Psychological Bulletin*, 104:53–69.

Hymowitz, and Schellhardt. (April 24, 1986). *Wall Street Journal*, sec. 4, p. 1.

Inman, C. (1996). Friendships between men: Closeness in doing. In J. T. Wood (Ed.), *Gendered Relationships*, 95–110. Mountain View, CA: Mayfield.

Irigaray, Luce. (1987). L'ordre sexuel du discours. *Langages,* vol. 85. Cited in D. Cameron (1992), *Feminism in Linguistic Theory.* London: MacMillan.

Irvine, J. J. (1986). Teacher-student interactions: Effects of student, race, sex, and grade level. *Journal of Educational Psychology*, 78(1): 14–21.

Jacobs, J. A., and Steinberg, R. J. (1995). Further evidence on compensating differentials and the gender gap in wages. In J. A. Jacobs (Ed.), *Gender Inequality at Work*, 93–114. Thousand Oaks, CA: Sage Publications.

Jamieson, K. H. (1995). *Beyond the Double Bind: Women and Leadership.* New York: Oxford University Press.

Johnson, F. L. (1996). Friendships among women: Closeness in dialogue. In J. T. Wood (Ed.), *Gendered Relationships*, 79–94. Mountain View, CA: Mayfield.

_____. (1989). Women's culture and communication: An analytic perspective. In C. M. Lont and S. A. Friedley (Eds.), *Beyond Boundaries: Sex and Gender Diversity in Communication*, 301–16. Fairfax, VA: George Mason University Press.

_____. (1980). Questions and role responsibility in four professional meetings. *Anthropological Linguistics*, 22:66–76.

Jones, G. M., and Wheatley, J. (1990). Gender differences in teacher-student interactions in science classrooms. *Journal of Research in Science Training*, 27(9): 861–74.

Jones, S. E. (1994). *The Right Touch: Understanding and Using the Language of Physical Contact.* Cresskill, NJ: Hampton Press.

Kanter, R. M. (1977). Some effects of proportions on group life: Skewed sex ratios and responses to token women. *American Journal of Sociology*, 82:965–90.

Keegan, P. (August 6, 1989). Playing favorites. *New York Times*, 4A; 26.

Keen, S. (1991). *The Fire in the Belly: On Being a Man.* New York: Bantam Books.

Keller, E. F. (September-October 1983). Feminism as an analytic tool for the study of science. *Academe.* Bulletin of the American Association of University Professors.

Kenkel, W. F. (1963). Observational studies of husband-wife interaction in family decision-making. In Marvin Sussman (Ed.), *Sourcebook in Marriage and the Family*, 144–56. Boston: Houghton Mifflin.

Kennedy, C. W. (1980). Patterns of verbal interruption among women and men in groups. Paper presented at the Third Annual Conference on Communication, Language, and Gender. Lawrence, Kansas.

Kennedy, C. W., and Camden, C. T. (1983). A new look at interruptions. *Western Journal of Speech Communication*, 43:45–48.

Keohane, N. O. (1981). Speaking from silence: Women and the science of politics. In E. Langland and W. Grove (Eds.), *A Feminist Perspective in the Academy*. Chicago: University of Chicago Press.

Kessler, R. C., and McRae, J., Jr. (April 1982). The effect of wives' employment on the mental health of married men and women. *Journal of Health and Social Behavior*, 47:216–27.

Kilborn, P. T. (March 16, 1995). Women and minorities still face glass ceiling. *New York Times*, C22.

Kimmel, Michael. (1987). *Changing Men: New Directions in Research on Men and Masculinity*. Newburg, CA: Sage Publications.

Kinsman, R. (1987). *The Telecommuters*. New York: John Wiley & Sons.

Knapp, M. L., and Hall, J. A. (1997). *Nonverbal Communication in Human Interaction*, 4th ed. Fort Worth, TX: Holt, Rinehart, and Winston.

Kramer, C. (1974). Stereotypes of women's speech: The word from cartoons. *Journal of Popular Culture*, 8:624–30.

Kramarae, C. (1981). *Women and Men Speaking*. Rowley, MA: Newbury House.

_____. (1992). Harrassment and everyday life. In L.F. Rakow (Ed.), *Women Making Meaning: New Feminist Directions in Communication*. New York: Routledge.

Labov, W. (1972). *Language in the Inner City: Studies in the Black English Vernacular*. Philadelphia: University of Pennsylvania Press.

LaFrance, M., and Henley, N. M. (1994). On oppressing hypotheses: Or differences in nonverbal sensitivity revisited. In H. L. Radke and H. J. Stam (Eds.), *Power/Gender: Social Relations in Theory and Practice*, 287–311. Thousand Oaks, CA: Sage Publications.

Ladd, R. D. (1980). *The Structure of Intonation Meaning: Evidence from English*. Bloomington: The University of Indiana Press.

Lakoff, R. (1975). *Language and Woman's Place*. New York: Harper & Row.

Leaska, M. A. (Ed.). (1984). *The Virginia Woolf Reader*. Orlando, FL: Harcourt, Brace, Jovanovich.

Leathers, D. (1986). *Successful Nonverbal Communication*. New York: Macmillan.

Lee, C. (November, 1994). The feminization of management. *Training and Development*, 25–31.

Leet-Pellegrini, H. M. (1980). Conversational dominance as a function of gender and expertise. In H. Giles, W. P. Robinson, and P. M. Smith (Eds.), *Language: Social Psychological Perspectives*, 97–104. New York: Pergammon Press.

Lerner, E. (1986). Family structure, occupation patterns and support for women's suffrage. In J. Friedlander et al. (Eds.), *Women in Culture and Politics: A Century of Change*. Bloomington: Indiana University Press.

Lesch, C. L. (1994). Observing theory in practice: Sustaining consciousness in a coven. In L. Frey (Ed.), *Group Communication in Context: Studies of Natural Groups*, 57–82. Hillsdale, NJ: Lawrence Erlbaum.

Levant, R. F. (1996). Reconstructing masculinity: The genesis and remediation of normative male Alexithymia. Paper presented at the American Psychological Association annual convention, Toronto, August 9–13.

Levine, L., and Crockett, H. J., Jr. (1979). Modal and modish pronunciation: Some sex differences in speech. In W. C. McCormack and S. A. Wurm (Eds.), *Language and Society: Anthropological Issues*, 207–20. The Hague: Mouton.

Lewin, T. (March 2, 1996). Child care in conflict with job. *New York Times*, 8.

Lombardo, J. P. (1986). Interaction of sex and sex role response to violations of preferred seating arrangements. *Sex Roles*, 15:173–83.

Longmire, L., and Merrill, L. (1998). *Untying the Tongue: Power, Gender, and the Word*. Westport, CO: Greenwood Press.

MacKinnon, C. (1979). *Sexual Harassment of Working Women*. New Haven: Yale University Press.

McConnell-Ginet, S. (1983). Intonation in a man's world. In B. Thorne, C. Kramarae, and N. M. Henley (Eds.), *Language, Gender and Society*, 69–88. Rowley, MA: Newbury House.

McConnell-Ginet, S., Borker, R., and Furman, N. (Eds.). (1980). *Women and Language in Literature and Society*. New York: Praeger.

McIntyre, S., Mohbert, D. J., and Posner, B. Z. (1980). Preferential treatment in preselection decisions according to sex and race. *Academy of Management Journal*, 23:738–49.

McQuarrie, F. A. (November-December, 1994). Telecommuting: Who really benefits? *Business Horizons*, 79–83.

Mahar, M. (April, 1993). The truth about women's pay. *Working Woman*, 52–55; 100–102.

Major, B. (1987). Gender, justice, and the psychology of entitlement. In P. Shaver and C. Hendrick (Eds.), *Sex and Gender*, 124–48. Newbury Park, CA: Sage Publications.

Maltz, D., and Borker, R. (1982). A cultural approach to male-female miscommunications. In J. J. Gumperz (Ed.), *Language and Social Identity*, 196–216. Cambridge, England: Cambridge University Press.

Marini, M. M., and Brinton, M. (1984). Sex typing in occupational socialization. In B. F. Reskin (Ed.), *Sex Segregation in the Workplace: Trends, Explanations, Remedies*. Washington: National Academy Press.

Markoff, J. (February 13, 1989). Computing in America: A masculine mystique. *New York Times*, 1.

Marlatt, G. A. (1970). A comparison of vicarious and direct reinforcement control of verbal behavior in an interview setting. *Journal of Personality and Social Psychology*, 16:695–703.

Martin, W. (Ed.). (1972). *American Sisterhood: Writings of the Feminist Movement from Colonial Times to the Present.* New York: Harper & Row.

Martinez, M. (1992). Interest enhancements to science experiments: Interactions with student gender. *Journal of Research in Science Teaching,* 29(2): 167–77.

Mattingly, I. (1966). Speaker variation and vocal tract size. Paper presented at the Acoustical Society of America. Abstract in *Journal of Acoustical Society of America,* 39:12–19.

Merrill, L. (1998). *When Romeo Was a Woman: Charlotte Cushman and Her Circle of Female Spectators.* Ann Arbor: University of Michigan Press.

Merrill, L., and Quirk, D. (1994). Gender, Media, and Militarism. In L. H. Turner and H. M. Sterk (Eds.), *Differences That Make a Difference: Examining the Assumptions in Gender Research.* Westport, CT: Bergin & Garvey.

Milroy, L. (1980). *Language and Social Networks.* Baltimore, MD: University Park Press.

Montgomery, B., and Norton, R. W. (1981). Sex differences and similarities in communicator style. *Communication Monographs,* 48:121–32.

Morrison, A. M., White, R. P., Van Velsor, E., and The Center for Creative Leadership. (1992). *Breaking the Glass Ceiling: Can Women Reach the Top of America's Largest Corporations?* 2d ed. Reading, MA: Addison-Wesley Publication Co.

Mulac, A., Wiemann, J. M., Widenmann, S. J., and Gibson, T. W. (1988). Male/female language differences in same-sex and mixed-sex dyads: The gender-linked language effect. *Communication Monographs,* 55:315–35.

Newcombe, N., and Arnkoff, D. B. (1979). Effects of speech style and sex of speaker on person perception. *Journal of Personality and Social Psychology,* 37:1293–1303.

Newton, M. W., (1989) Women and pension coverage, *The American Woman 1988–1989: A Status Report,* Rix, S. ed. New York: W. W. Norton and Co.

Nichols, P. (1980). Women in their speech communities. In S. McConnell-Ginet, R. Borker, and N. Furman (Eds.), *Women and Language in Literature and Society,* 140–49. New York: Praeger.

_____. (1983). Linguistic options and choices for Black women in the rural South. In B. Thorne, C. Kramarae, and N. M. Henley (Eds.), (1983), *Language, Gender, and Society, 54–68.* Rowley, MA: Newbury House.

Nichols, R. (1948). Unpublished dissertation State University of Iowa. Cited in L. Steil, L. L. Barker, and K. Watson. (1983). *Effective Listening: Key to Your Success.* Reading, MA: Addison-Wesley.

Nierenberg, G. I., and Calero, H. H. (1971). *How to Read a Person Like a Book.* New York: Hawthorne.

O'Barr, W. M., and Atkins, B. (1980). Women's language or powerless language? In S. McConnell-Ginet, R. Borker, and N. Furman (Eds.),

Women and Language in Literature and Society, 93–110. New York: Praeger.

Ong, W. (1972). Review of Brian Vickes' Classical Rhetoric in English Poetry. Published in *College English* (February).

Paetzold, R. L., and O'Leary-Kelly, A. M. (1993). Organizational communication and the legal dimensions of hostile work environment sexual harassment. In G. L. Kreps (Ed.), *Sexual Harassment: Communication Implications*, 63–77. Cresskill, NJ: Hampton Press.

Pearson, J. C., and West, R. (1991). An initial investigation of the effects of gender on student questions in the classroom: Developing a descriptive base. *Communication Education*, 40:22–32.

Pedro, J. D., Wolleat, P., Fennema, E., and Becker, A. D. (Summer 1981). Election of high school mathematics by females and males: Attributions and attitudes. *American Educational Research*, 18:207–18.

Peltz, W. (December, 1990). Can girls + science – stereotypes = success? *The Science Teacher*, 57(9): 44–49.

Penelope, J. (1990). *Speaking Freely: Unlearning the Lies of the Fathers' Tongues*, New York: Teachers College Press.

Piliavin, J. A., and Martin, R. R. (1978). The effects of the sex composition of groups on style of social interaction. *Sex Roles*, 4:281–96.

Pollitt, K. (October 6, 1995). Why boys don't play with dolls. *New York Times Sunday Magazine*, 46; 48.

Postman, N. M. (1995). *The End of Education*. New York: Alfred A. Knopf.

Powell, G. N. (1993). *Women and Men in Management*, 2d ed. Newbury Park, CA: Sage Publications.

Putnam, L. L. (1983). Lady you're trapped: Breaking out of conflict cycles. In J. J. Pilotta (Ed.), *Women in Organizations: Barriers and Breakthroughs*, 39–53. Prospect Heights, IL: Waveland Press.

Rakow, L. W. (Ed.). (1992). *Women Making Meaning in New Directions in Communication*. New York: Routledge.

Raty, H., and Snellman, L. (1992). Does gender make any difference?: Common sense conceptions of intelligence. *Social Behavior and Personality*, 20(1): 23–34.

Reisman, J. M. (1990). Intimacy in same-sex friendships. *Sex roles*, 23:65–82.

Remick, H. (1984). Major issues in *a priori* applications. In H. Remick (Ed.), *Comparable Worth and Wage Discrimination: Technical Possibilities and Political Realities*, 109–47. Washington: National Committee on Pay Equity.

Roberts, S. (April 27, 1995). Women's work: What's new, what isn't. *New York Times*, A12.

Roman, C., Juhasz, S., and Miller, C. (1994). *The Woman and Language Debate: A Sourcebook*. New Brunswick, NJ: Rutgers University Press.

Rosenfeld, L. B., and Jarrard, M. W. (1986). Student coping mechanisms in sexist and nonsexist professors' classes. *Communication Education*, 35:157–62.

Rosenthal, R., and DePaulo, B. (1979). Sex differences in accommodation in nonverbal communication. In R. Rosenthal (Ed.), *Skill in Nonverbal Communication: Individual Differences*. Cambridge, MA: Oelgeschlager, Gunn and Hain.

Rosenthal, R., Hall, J., DiMatteo, M. R., Rogers, R. S., and Archer, D. (1979). *Sensitivity to Nonverbal Communication: The PONS Test*. Baltimore, MD: Johns Hopkins University Press.

Ross, J. M. (1994). *What Men Want: Mothers, Fathers, and Manhood*. Cambridge: Harvard University Press.

Rubin, L. B. (1983). *Intimate Strangers*. New York: Harper & Row.

_____. (1985). *Just Friends: The Role of Friendship in Our Lives*. New York: Harper & Row.

Ruether, R. (1981). Feminist critique in religious studies. In E. Langland and W. Grove (Eds.), *A Feminist Perspective in the Academy*. Chicago: University of Chicago Press.

Ryan, M. P. (1975). *Womanhood in America*. New York: Franklin Watts.

Sachs, J., Liberman, P., and Erickson, D. (1973). Anatomical and cultural determinants of male and female speech. In R. W. Shuy and R. W. Fasold (Eds.), *Language Attitudes: Current Trends and Prospects*. Washington, DC: Georgetown University Press.

Sadker, M., and Sadker, D. (1994). *Failing at Fairness: How America's Schools Cheat Girls*. New York: Charles Scribner's Sons.

_____. (March 1985). Sexism in the schoolroom of the '80s. *Psychology Today*, 54–57.

_____. (1984). *Year 3: Final Report: Promoting Effectiveness in Classroom Instruction*. Washington: National Institute of Education.

Sandberg, D. E., Ehrhardt, A. A., Mellins, C. A., Ince, S. E., and Meyer-Bahlburg, H. F. L. (1987). The influence of individual and family characteristics upon career aspirations of girls during childhood and adolescence. *Sex roles*, 16:649–68.

Sanders, J. S. (1984). The computer: Male, female, or androgynous? *The Computing Teacher*, 11(8): 31–34.

Sanders, J. et al., (1985). Personal space amongst Arabs and Americans. *International Journal of Psychology*, 20(1): 13–17.

Sandler, B. (1991). Women faculty at work in the classroom, or why it still hurts to be a woman in labor. *Communication Education*, 40:6–15.

Schor, J. B. (1991). *The Overworked American: The Unexpected Decline of Leisure*. New York: Basic Books.

Shapiro, L. (May 28, 1990). Guns and dolls: Nature or nurturance? *Newsweek*, 56–65.

Shaw, L. (1996). *Telecommute! Go to Work without Leaving Home.* New York: John Wiley & Sons.

Shuter, R. (1976). Nonverbal communication: Proxemics and tactility in Latin America. *Journal of Communication,* 26(3): 46–52.

Shuy, R. W., Wolfram, W. A., and Riley, W. K. (1967). Linguistic correlates of a social stratification in Detroit speech. Final Report, Project 6–347. Washington, DC: Office of Education.

Sieburg, E., and Larson, C. (1971). Dimensions of interpersonal response. Paper presented to the International Communication Association, Phoenix, Arizona.

Silveira, J. (February 1972). Thoughts on the politics of touch. *Women's Press,* 1:13.

Snyder, D. P. (March-April, 1996). The revolution in the workplace: What's happening to our jobs? *The Futurist,* 15–17.

Spain, D. (1992). *Gendered Spaces.* Chapel Hill: University of North Carolina Press.

Span, P. (May, 1995). A man can take 'maternity' leave . . . and love it. *Redbook,* 51:54; 56.

Spender, D. (1980). *Man-made Language.* London: Routledge & Kegan Paul.

Steckler, N. A., and Cooper, W. E. (1980). Sex differences in color naming of unisex apparel. *Anthropological Linguistics,* 22:373–81.

Steinberg, R. J. (1990). The social construction of skill. *Work and Occupations,* 17:449–82.

Steinem, G. (1983). *Outrageous Acts and Everyday Rebellions.* New York: Holt, Rinehart and Winston.

Steinhauer, J. (March 27, 1997). If the boss is out of line, what's the legal boundary. *New York times,* D1; D4.

Stewart, L. P. (1982). Women in management: Implications for communication researchers. Paper presented at the Eastern Communication Association, Hartford, Connecticut.

Stockard, J., and Johnson, M. M. (1980). *Sex Roles: Sex Inequality and Sex Role Development.* Englewood Cliffs, NJ: Prentice-Hall.

Stock-Morton, P. (1991). Finding our own ways: Different paths to women's history in the United States. In K. Offen et al. (Eds.) *Writing Women's History: International Perspectives.* Bloomington: Indiana University Press.

Stoltenberg, John. (1990). *Refusing to be a Man: Essays on Sex and Justice.* New York: Penguin, Meridian.

Stone, J., and Bachner, J. (1977). *Speaking Up: A Book for Every Woman Who Wants to Speak Effectively.* New York: McGraw-Hill.

Strodtbeck, F., James, R. M., and Hawkins, C. (1957). Social status in jury deliberations. *American Sociological Review,* 22:718.

Strodtbeck, F., and Mann, R. D. (1956). Sex role differentiation in jury deliberations. *Sociometry,* 19:3–11.

Stutman, R. K. (1987). Witness disclaiming during examination. *Journal of the American Forensic Association*, 23:96–101.

Swacker, M. (1976). Women's behavior at learned and professional conferences. In B. L. Dubois and I. Crouch (Eds.), *The Sociology of the Language of American Women*, 155–60. San Antonio, TX: Trinity University.

Swain, S. (1989). Covert intimacy: Closeness in men's friendships. In B. J. Risman and P. Schwartz (Eds.), *Gender in Intimate Relationships*, 71–86. Belmont, CA: Wadsworth.

Swisher, K. (February 14–20, 1994). Corporations are seeing the light on harassment. *Washington Post National Weekly Edition*, 21.

Tannen, D. (1987). *That's Not What I Meant! How Conversation Style Makes or Breaks Relationships*. New York: Ballatine.

_____. (1990). *You Just Don't Understand: Women and Men in Conversation*. New York: William Morrow, Ballentine.

_____. (1994). *Gender and Discourse*. New York: Oxford University Press.

Tarvis, C. (1992). *The Mismeasure of Woman*. New York: Simon & Schuster.

Tarvis, C., and Wade, C. (1984). *The Longest War: Sex Differences in Perspective*, 2d ed. Orlando, FL: Harcourt, Brace, Jovanovich.

Terango, L. (1966). Pitch and duration characteristics of the oral reading of males on a masculinity-femininity dimension. *Journal of Speech and Hearing Research*, 9:580–90.

Thomas, B. (1989). Differences of sex and sects. In J. Coates and D. Cameron (Eds.), *Women in Their Speech Communities: New Perspectives on Language and Sex*. London: Longman.

Thorne, B. (1986). Girls and boys together . . . but mostly apart: Gender arrangements in elementary schools. In W. W. Hartrup and Z. Rubin (Eds.), *Relationships and Development*. Hillsdale, NJ: Lawrence Erlbaum.

_____. (1990). Children and Gender: Constructions of Difference. In D. Rhode (Ed.), *Theoretical Perspectives on Sexual Difference*. New Haven: Yale University Press.

_____. (1993). *Gender Play: Girls and Boys in School*. New Brunswick, NJ: Rutgers University Press.

Thorne, B., and Henley, N. M. (Eds.). (1975). *Language and Sex: Differences and Dominance*. Rowley, MA: Newbury House.

Tong, R. (1984). *Women, Sex, and the Law*. Savage, MA: Rowman & Littlefield.

Trudgill, P . (1975). Sex, covert prestige and linguistic change in the urban British English of Norwich. In B. Thorne and N. M. Henley (Eds.), *Language and Sex: Differences and Dominance*, 88–104. Rowley, MA: Newbury House.

Truth, S. (1878). *Narrative of Sojourner Truth, A Bondswoman of Olden Time*. Compiled by Olive Gilbert. Reprint, New York: Arno Press, 1968.

Turner, L. H., Dindia, K., and Pearson, J. C. (1995). An investigation of female/male verbal behaviors in same-sex and mixed-sex conversations. *Communication Reports*, 8:86–96.

Uchitelle, L. (November 24, 1990). Women's push into work force seems to have reached plateau. The *New York Times*, A1.

U.S. Department of Labor (February, 1989). Bureau of Labor Statistics. *Handbook of Labor Statistics*, Table 5, 25–30.

_____. (May, 1992). Bureau of Labor Statistics. *Employment and Earnings*, 39:5, Table A-22, 29.

Valentine, G. (March, 1997). 'My son's a bit ditzy.' 'My wife's a bit soft': Gender, children and cultures of parenting. *Gender, Place and Culture*, 4(1): 37–62.

Veblen, T. (1899). *Theory of the Leisure Class.* Reprint, New York: New American Library, 1953.

Watson, C. (1994). Gender differences in negotiating behavior and outcomes: Fact or artifact? In A. Taylor and J. Beinstein Miller (Eds.), *Conflict and Gender*, 191–209. Cresskill, NJ: Hampton Press.

West, C. (1984). When the doctor is a "lady": Power, status and gender in physician-patient encounters. Cited in D. Cameron, *Feminism in Linguistic Theory*, p. 71. London: MacMillan, 1992.

_____. (1994). Rethinking 'sex differences' in conversational topics: It's not what they say but how they say it. In C. Roman, S. Juhasz, and C. Miller (Eds.), *The Woman and Language Debate: A Soucebook*. New Brunswick, NJ: Rutgers University Press.

West, C., and Garcia, A. (1988). Conversational shift work: A study of topical transitions between women and men. *Social Problems*, 35:551–75.

West, C., and Zimmerman, D. H. (1983). Small insults: A study of interruptions in cross-sex conversations between unacquainted persons. In B. Thorne, C. Kramarae, and N. M. Henley (Eds.), *Gender, Language and Society*. Rowley, MA: Newbury House.

Whiting, B. B., and Edwards, C. P. (1988). *Children of Different Worlds: The Formation of Social Behavior*. Cambridge: Harvard University Press.

Wilden, A. (1987). *Man and Woman, War and Peace: The Strategist's Companion*. New York: Routledge and Kegan Paul.

Wilkins, B. M., and Anderson, P. A. (1991). Gender differences and similarities in management communication: A meta-analysis. *Communication Quarterly*, 3:6–35.

Williams, D. G. (1985). Gender, masculinity-femininity, and emotional intimacy in same-sex friendship. *Sex Roles*, 12:587–600.

Williams, J. E., and Best, D. L. (1982). *Measuring Sex Stereotypes: A Thirty Nation Study*. Beverly Hills: Sage Publications.

Willis, F. (1966). Initial speaking distance as a function of the speaker's relationship. *Psychonomic Science*, 5:221–22.

Willis, F., and Williams, S. J. (1976). Simultaneous talking in conversations and sex of speakers. *Perceptual and Motor Skills*, 43:1067–70.

Wilson, P. R. (1968). Perceptual distortion of height as a function of ascribed academic status. *Journal of Social Psychology*, 74:97–192.

Wolf, N. (1991). *The Beauty Myth: How Images of Beauty are Used Against Women*. New York: Morrow.

Wolfram, W. (1969). *A Sociolinguistic Description of Detroit Negro Speech*. Washington, DC: Center for Applied Linguistics.

Wood, J. T. (Spring, 1992). Gender and moral voice: Moving from woman's nature to standpoint epistemology. *Women's Studies in Communication*, 15:1, 1–24.

_____. (1993). Naming and interpreting sexual harassment: A conceptual framework for scholarship. In G. L. Kreps (Ed.), *Sexual Harassment: Communication Implications*, 9–26. Cresskill, NJ: Hampton Press.

_____. (1994). *Gendered Lives: Communication, Gender, and Culture*. Belmont, CA: Wadsworth.

Wood, J. T., and Inman, C. C. (August, 1993). In a different mode: Masculine styles of communicating closeness. *Journal of Applied Communication Research*, 2(3): 279–95.

Woolf, Virginia. (1929). "A Room of One's Own." In M. Leaska (Ed.), *The Virginia Woolf Reader*, 168–88. Orlando, FL: Harcourt, Brace, Jovanovich, 1984.

Young, M., and Willmott, P. (1973). *The Symmetrical Family*. New York: Pantheon.

Zimmerman, D., and West, C. (1975). Sex roles, interruptions, and silences in conversation. In B. Thorne and N. Henley (Eds.), *Language and Sex: Difference and Dominance*, 105–29. Rowley, MA: Newbury House.

Zuckerman, M., DeFrank, R. S., Spiegel, N. H., and Larrance, D. T. (1982). Masculinity-femininity and the encoding of nonverbal cues. *Journal of Personality and Social Psychology*, 42:548–56.

Index

Abolitionists, Grimke sisters as, 7
Activists, female, 7–9
African Americans. *See* Ethnicity;
    Race
Allan, J. M., 5
Allen, E., 39
Anderson, P., 98
Androcentrism, 71–72
Appearance. *See also* Artifactual
    messages
    hiring and, 93
    teacher attention to, 82
Arliss, L., 42
Arnkoff, D., 30
Articulation, 20–23
Artifactual messages, 63–64
Assertiveness, sexual harassment
    and, 106
Atkins, B., 29–30
Austin, W., 24
Authoritativeness. *See also* Power
    of male speakers, 14–15

Bachner, J., 11
Backlash, toward women and work,
    74–75
Beattie, M., 41
Beauty. *See* Appearance
Beck, A., 41
Behaviors. *See also* Sexual
    harassment; Stereotypes; Verbal
    behaviors; Vocal behaviors
    in classrooms, 80–83
    of effective management, 98–100

gender and, 2, 12–13, 120–21
    verbal, 19–20, 28–35
    vocal, 19–28
Bem, S., 71, 112
Bernard, J., 72
Berryman-Fink, C., 102, 108, 109
Best, D., 73
Betts, M., 117
Bias, in hiring, 94
Bingham, S., 105
Biology, male/female roles and, 71,
    121, 122
Black English, 21
Blackwell, H., 8
Blake, S., 96
Blumer, H., 90
Blumstein, P., 112
Bochner, S., 55
Body Politics (Henley), 62
Borisoff, 32, 60, 82, 105
Borker, R., 13, 42
Boys. *See also* Gender; Gender
    differences; Masculinity; Men
    behavior expected of, 73
Bredin, A., 98
Brend, R., 26
Buck, R., 60
Butler, J., 51

Calero, H. H., 59
Camden, C., 41
Cameron, D., 10, 21, 32
Careers. *See also* Child care; Family;
    Workplace

women's attitudes toward, 76–79
"women's work" and, 90–92
Carlsmith, J., 61
Change. *See* Stereotypes
Child care
responsibility for, 77–78, 109–15
working at home and, 117
Child development, language use
and, 4
Chira, S., 110
Civil Rights Act (1964), sexual
harassment and, 102
Clair, R., 104, 106
Class (socioeconomic)
gender norms and, 73–74
gestures and, 63
touch and, 56
Classroom. *See* Education
Clothing. *See also* Appearance
and artifactual messages, 63–64
power and, 53, 54
Cohen, T., 112
Collingwood, H. 98
Colloquial speech, 21
Communication
defined, 1–2
sexual harassment and, 103
Communication styles. *See also*
Gender
changing, 121–22
gender-stereotyped, 108
of women and men, 3–4
in workplace, 100
Compliance, of women, 11
Compound requests, 33
Confirmation, tag questions for, 32
Confrontation, sexual harassment
and, 106
Connotation, vocal behaviors and, 28
Cooper, P., 34
Courtright, J., 38
Cox, T., 96
Credibility. *See* Femininity
Crockett, H., 21

Crosby, F., 29
Crouch, I., 32
Culture. *See also* Class; Roles;
Socialization
gender norms and, 73–74
gestures and, 63
as habit, 72
personal space and, 54–55
Curt, C., 62

Dass, K., 43
Deaux, K., 47
de Beauvoir, S., 11–12, 13, 119
Decoding, of nonverbal
communication, 64–66
Deficit theory, in gender difference
research, 46
Demeanor, 63
DeWine, S., 97
Dialects, 28
Dill, B. T., 74
Dindia, 39, 41
Disclaimers, 31
Disconfirming responses, 45–46
Discrimination
in hiring, 92–94
salary practices and, 95
Diversity, workplace issues and, 96
Dolphin, C. Z., 54
Dominance
communicative behaviors and, 43–
47
by male speakers, 15
nonverbal aspects of stereotypes
and, 16
sexual harassment and, 102–9
Domineeringness, 38
Dress. *See* Clothing
Dual culture approach, to gender
studies, 100–101
Dualism, 70–72
Duberman, L., 10
Dubois, B., 32

Dyadic communication, 35–36. *See also* Interactions

Eagly, 93, 98, 99
Edelsky, C., 27
Edgar, T., 39
Education. *See also* Language training
   articulation and, 21–22
   changing gender stereotypes, 120
   gender and subjects in, 84–85
   male-female experiences with, 80–86
   about sexual harassment issues, 107–9
Effeminacy, male emotionalism and, 14
Ehrenreich, B., 110
Eisler, R., 98
Ellsworth, P., 61
Ellyson, S., 62
Ely, R., 110
Eman-Wheeless, V., 102
Emotionalism
   of men, 14
   of women, 12–13
Emotions. *See* Emotionalism; Facial expressions; Self-disclosure
Employers. *See also* Workplace
   hiring bias of, 94
Empowerment. *See* Power
End of Education, The (Postman), 80
English, D., 110
English language, 21
Equal Employment Opportunity Commission, 97
   sexual harassment and, 103
Erickson, D., 23
Essentialism, gender stereotypes and, 71
Ethics, sexual harassment and, 104
Ethnicity, 4
   gender norms and, 73–74
   self-disclosure and, 39

Expectations, performance and, 98
Expletives, 35
Eye contact, 61–62

Facial expressions, 58–61
   decoding, 65
Faludi, S., 74
Family. *See also* Home; Roles; Socialization
   child care and, 109–15
   men's attitudes toward, 112–13
   nuclear, 75–76
   roles of men and women in, 74–79
   symmetry of responsibility in, 111–12
Family and Medical Leave Act (1993), 109
Family and Work Institute, 111, 115
Family leaves, 113–15
Fathers. *See* Family; Husbands; Men
Feedback, 45. *See also* Minimal responses
Femininity. *See also* Stereotypes; erbal behaviors; Vocal behaviors
   facial expressions and, 60
   stereotypes of, 6–12, 120
Fishman, P., 14, 32, 37, 42
Friedman, D., 115
Friendships, self-disclosure and, 38–40

Gabor, A., 112
Gaines, S., 39
Gal, S., 5
Gays, self-disclosure and, 39–40
Gaze, 61–62
Gender. *See also* Behaviors; Discrimination; Education; Men; Nonverbal communication; Stereotypes; Women; specific issues
   dual culture approach to, 100–101
   feminine stereotypes and, 6–12
   management behaviors and, 98–99

masculine stereotypes and, 12–15
nonverbal communication and,
    51–66
role of, 2–4
scripts and, 69–87
socialization and, 38–39
student performance and, 83–86
in virtual office, 115–17
in workplace, 89–117
Gender differences, 3
communicative behaviors and, 43–
    47, 108–9
and "correct" speech, 21–23
Gendered Spaces (Spain), 115
"Genderlect," 18
Gender norms, 73–74
culturally-specific, 74–75
Gerson, K., 112, 113
Gestures, 63
Gilligan, C., 15
Gilman, C. P., 69, 71
Girls. *See also* Femininity; Gender;
    Gender differences; Women
behavior expected of, 73
Gleason, J. B., 41, 72
Goffman, E., 24, 51
Grammar, 21
Greif, 41, 73
Grimke sisters, 7
Grosz, E., 64
Gullah speakers, 22

*Habits of Good Society: A Handbook
    for Ladies and Gentlemen,* 63
Hahn, 60, 82
Halberstadt, A., 58
Hall, J., 53, 56, 60, 62, 64–65, 66
Hall, E. T., 72
Harlan, A., 99, 111
Hartford, B., 21
Height, 57–58
Heilbrun, C., 5
Heilman, M., 92
Henley, N., 28, 56, 60, 62, 65

Henrique, D., 94
Henson, A., 61
Herndon, S., 107, 108
Hill, A., 102–3
Hiring practices, gender and, 92–94
Hite, S., 42
Hochschild, A. R., 59, 78, 111, 112,
    117
Home. *See also* Family;
    Socialization; Virtual office
    socialization in, 72–73
Homophobia. *See* Gender;
    Stereotypes
Homosexuals. *See* Gays
hooks, b., 90
Husbands. *See also* Child care;
    Home; Men
roles of, 8–9
Hutchinson, A., 6, 10
Hymowitz, 98

Initiation of topics, 37–38
Inman, C., 39
Interactions
interruptions and overlaps in, 40–
    42
pitch and, 24
self-disclosure in, 38–40
space in, 53
talk time and, 36–37
topic initiation and selection in, 37–
    38
verbal and vocal behaviors in, 35–
    47
Intercultural communication, gaze
    and, 62
Internalization, of stereotypes, 10
Interruptions, 40–42, 44
by fathers, 73
Intimacy. *See* Self-disclosure; Space;
    Touch
Intonation, 25–28
Irigaray, L., 34
Irvine, J. J., 81

Isolation, in virtual office, 116–17

Jacobs, J., 96, 97
Jobs. *See* Workplace
Johnson, B., 98
Johnson, F., 32, 39
Johnson, M., 112
Jones, G., 85

Karau, S., 98
Keller, E. F., 11
Kennedy, C. W., 41
Keohane, N. O., 9
Kessler, R. C., 112
Kessler-Harris, A., 74
Knapp, 53, 56, 62
Kramarae, C., 20, 103
Kramer, C., 28

Labor force. *See* Workplace
Labov, W., 21
"Ladylike" behavior, 10–12, 51, 63
La France, M., 60
Lakoff, R., 10, 26–27, 28, 31, 33
Language training, of men, 12–13
Larson, C., 45
Learned behavior, 53
Leaska, M. A., 89
Leaves of absence. *See also* Family
    leaves
workplace disparities and, 96
Lee, C., 98
Leet-Pellegrini, H., 36
Lerner, E., 99
Levine, L., 21
Lieberman, P., 23
Listening, 44–45. *See also* Behaviors
    by men and women, 13–14
Lombardo, 55
Longmire, L., 20

MacKinnon, C., 108
Mahar, M., 95
Major, B., 47, 95

Maltz, D., 13, 42
Management. *See also* Child care;
    Workplace
behaviors of effective, 98–100
disparity between men and women
    in, 101
flexible style of, 102
telecommuting and, 116
*Man-Made World, The: or, Our
    Androcentric Culture* (Gilman),
    69, 71
Marriage. *See also* Careers; Child
    care; Family
role of, 75–76
Masculinity. *See also* Stereotypes
facial expressions and, 60
stereotypes of, 12–15, 120
Mason, P., 6–7
Matching, speech and, 28–29
Maternity leave, 114
Mattingly, I., 23
Mattis, M., 101
McAlinden, F., 32
McConnell-Ginet, S., 26
McGoun, M., 106
McIntyre, S., 92
McRae, J., 112
Mediators, women as, 13
Men. *See also* Gender; Masculinity;
    Workplace; specific issues
attitudes toward family and work,
    112–13
educational practices and, 80–86
as homemakers, 113–14
roles in family, 77–78
Merrill, 20, 32
Messages. *See also* Nonverbal
    communication
of sexual harassment, 103–4
Millar, F., 38
Milroy, L., 21
Minimal responses, 42–43, 44–45
Minority groups, workplace barriers
    and, 101–2

Mohberg, D., 92
Morrison, A., 98, 110
Mothers. *See* Family; Wives; Women
Mott, L., 7–8

Negotiation, sexual harassment and,
106
Networking, telecommuting
limitations and, 116
Newcombe, N., 30
Nichols, P., 21
Nichols, R., 40, 42
Nierenberg, G. I., 59
Nine, J., 62
Nonverbal aspects of stereotypes, 16–
17
Nonverbal communication, 4
artifactual messages and, 63–64
decoding, 64–66
facial expressions as, 58–61
gaze and, 61–62
gender and, 51–66
gesture, demeanor, and, 63
height and, 57–58
space and, 52–55
touch and, 55–57
Norms. *See also* Culture; Gender;
Gender norms; Socialization
impact of violating, 11
performance and, 98
Nyquist, J., 29

O'Barr, W., 29–30
Occupations
articulation and, 21–22
pitch and, 24–25
O'Leary, K., 32
Ong, W. J., 12
Opposites, dualism and, 70
Organizational culture
appearance and, 93–94
performance and, 97–98
Overlaps, 40–42, 44

Paternity leave, 113–14
Penelope, J., 9, 37
Performance
and gender, 97–102
of students, by gender, 83–86
Phonetics, 21
Pitch, 23–25
rapid changes in, 27
Politeness, power and, 44
Pollitt, K., 73
PONS (Profile of Nonverbal
Sensitivity) Test, 65
Posner, B., 92
Postman, N., 80
Powell, G., 92, 94, 98, 110
Power. *See also* Facial expressions;
Nonverbal communication;
Space; Workplace
clothing and, 53, 54
communicative behaviors and, 44
decoding facial expressions and,
65–66
height and, 57–58
sexual harassment and, 102–9
stereotypes and, 9
Powerful language, 28
Professionals. *See also* Professions
studies of behaviors, 99–100
Professions. *See also* Careers;
Workplace
appearance and, 93–94
"feminine," 97
performance, gender, and, 97–102
Pronunciation, 21
Proxemics, 52–55
Pruett, K., 79
Public speaking, 5–9
by Grimke sisters, 7

Qualifiers, 29–30
Questions. *See also* Compound
requests; Tag questions
topic initiation, 37

Race
  facial expressions and, 58–59
  femininity and, 79
  self-confidence of girls by, 83
Rakow, L., 79
Raty, H., 84
Requests, compound, 33
Responses. *See also* Verbal
    behaviors; Vocal behaviors
  disconfirming, 45–46
  minimal, 42–43, 44–45
Rhetoric, 12–13
Riley, W., 21
Rogers-Millar, L., 38
Role division, 7
Roles. *See also* Stereotypes
  of adult women, 75
  of husbands and wives, 8–9
  traditional women's, 76–77
  of working men and women, 76–79
"Room of One's Own, A" (Woolf), 89,
    117
Rosenthal, R., 65
Rousseau, J. J., 19
Rubin, L., 40, 78

Sachs, J., 23
Sadker, D., 80, 81
Sadker, M., 80, 81
Saitta, M., 58
Salary practices, 95–97
Sanders, J., 54
Sandler, B., 81
Schellhardt, 98
Schneer, J., 96
School. *See also* Education
  socialization in, 69–87
Schwartz, P., 112
Scripts (gender), 69–87, 119–22
Self-confidence, of girls and boys, 83–
    84
Self-disclosure, 38–40
Self-effacing communication, 10–11
Seneca Falls Convention, 8

Sex and sexuality. *See also*
    Nonverbal communication;
    Sexual harassment
  eye contact and, 62
Sexism, in workplace, 90–91
Sex-roles, 55
Sexual harassment, 102–9
  and avoidance, 104–5
  and diffusion, 105
  training in avoidance of, 107–9
Shakespeare, W., 51
Shaw, L.,116
Shuter, R., 54
Shuy, R., 21
Sieburg, E., 45
Silence. *See* Talk time
Silveira, J., 53
Smiling, 58–60
Snellman, L., 84
Socialization
  gender, 38–39
  gendered scripts and, 69–87
  sex-traits, sex-roles, and, 72–79
Society, power and stereotypes in, 9,
    121
Socioeconomic class. *See* Class
Sociolinguistics, verbal constructs
    and, 28
Soft-spoken communication, 10
Space
  gender in schools and, 82–83
  nonverbal communication and,
    52–55
  sexual harassment and, 108
Spain, D., 115
Spanish-speaking people, gender
    and, 21
Speech, and group solidarity, 28–29
Speeches. *See* Public speaking
Spender, D., 36
Spirek, M., 106
Standard English, gender and use of,
    21
Standpoint theory, 121

Stanton, E. C., 7–8
Stanton, H. B., 8
Staring. *See* Gaze
Status. *See also* Class
    gaze and, 62
    touch and, 56
Steckler, N., 34
Steinberg, R., 96, 97
Steinem, G., 14
Stereotypes, 5–6. *See also* Gender;
        Scripts (gender); Verbal
        behaviors; Vocal behaviors
    biological essentialism and, 71
    change and, 119–22
    education and, 80–83, 84
    feminine, 6–10
    limitations of feminine, 10–12
    masculine, 12–15
    nonverbal aspects of, 16–17
    about pitch, 24–25
    professional performance in
        workplace and, 97–102
    sexual, 72
    social purposes of, 9
    workplace-related, 90–94, 99, 108–
        9
Stockard, J., 112
Stock-Morton, P., 89
Stone, J., 11
Stone, L., 8
Strodtbeck, F., 36
Students. *See also* Education
    assumptions about performance
        of, 83–86
    teaching styles toward, by gender,
        80–83
Submissiveness. *See also*
        Stereotypes
    nonverbal aspects of stereotypes,
        16
Success. *See also* Workplace
    women's and men's attitudes
        toward, 78

Tag questions, 31–33
Talk time, 36–37
Tannen, D., 41
Teaching. *See also* Education
    gender of students and, 80–83
Technology. *See also* Virtual office
    gender in classroom and, 85
Telecommuting, limitations of, 116–
    17
Terango, L., 26
Thomas, B., 22
Thomas, C., 103
Thorne, B., 27, 28, 56–57, 82
Tong, 103, 108
Topic initiation and selection, 37–38,
    44–45
Touch, 55–57
Training. *See also* Education
    in sexual harassment issues, 107–9
Trudgill, P., 21
Truth, S., 9

Valentine, G., 83
Van Velsor, E., 98
Veblen, T., 53
Verbal behaviors, 28–35
    compound requests and, 33
    disclaimers as, 30–31
    in interaction, 35–47
    interruptions, overlaps, and, 40–42
    qualifiers and, 29–30
    self-disclosure and, 38–40
    tag questions and, 31–33
    talk time and, 36–37
    topic initiation and selection, 37–
        38
    vocabulary differences and, 34–35
Victims, of sexual harassment, 103–6
Virtual office
    gender in, 115–17
    limitations of, 116–17
Vocabulary, 28
    gender differences and, 34–35
Vocal behaviors, 19–28

articulation as, 20–23
in interaction, 35–47
intonation and, 25–28
pitch as, 23–25
vocalizers, minimal responses,
  and, 42–43
Vocalizers, 42–43
Vulnerability, 39

Wages. *See* Salary practices
Watson, 100
Weiss, C. L., 99, 111
Welsh speakers, 22
West, C., 14, 38, 41–42
Wheatley, J., 85
White, R. P., 98
Whites. *See* Ethnicity; Race
Wilkins, B., 98
Williams, J., 73
Willis, F., 53
Willmott, P., 112
Wilson, P. R., 57
Winthrop, J., 6
Wives. *See also* Child care; Home;
  Women
  roles of, 8–9
Wolfram, W., 21
Women. *See also* Gender;
  Stereotypes; Workplace; specific
  issues
  assumptions about adult roles of,
    75
  educational practices and, 80–86
  feminine stereotypes and, 6–12
  limitations of feminine stereotypes
    and, 10–12

public speaking and, 5–6
  traditional roles of, 76–77
  in workforce, 74–75, 76
Women's rights movement, women
  as speakers and, 7–8
"Women's work," 90–92
Wood, J., 63, 103, 105, 121
Woolf, V., 89, 117
Work, role in men's lives, 113
Workforce, women and, 74–75, 76–
  79
Working-class speech, 22–23
Workplace. *See also* Family
  barriers to women and minorities
    in, 101–2
  career vs. personal commitments
    in, 110–11
  child care responsibilities and,
    109–15
  conditions in, 96–97
  family leave policies and, 113–15
  gender in, 89–117
  hiring practices in, 92–94
  professional performance and
    gender in, 97–102
  salary practices in, 95–97
  sexual harassment in, 102–9
  stereotyping by gender in, 90–92
  virtual office limitations and, 115–
    17

Yin/yang, 70
Young, M., 112

Zimmerman, D. H., 14, 41
Zuckerman, M., 60